Essential Dutch Grammar

By
HENRY R. STERN

Chairman, Department of Foreign Languages
The University of North Carolina at Asheville

DOVER PUBLICATIONS, INC.
NEW YORK

Essential Dutch Grammar is a new work, first published by
Dover Publications, Inc., in 1984.

The Essential Grammar series is prepared under the editorial supervision of R. A. Sorenson.

Manufactured in the United States of America
Dover Publications, Inc., 31 East 2nd Street, Mineola,
N.Y. 11501

Library of Congress Cataloging in Publication Data

Stern, Henry R.
  Essential Dutch grammar.

  Includes index.
    1. Dutch language—Grammar—1950–   2. Dutch
language—Text-books for foreign speakers—English.
I. Title.
PF112.S74 1984   439.3′182421   83-20593
ISBN 0-486-24675-2

CONTENTS

CONTENTS

INTRODUCTION

Essential Dutch Grammar is based on the assumption that you plan to spend a limited number of hours studying Dutch grammar and that your objective is simple everyday communication. This book is not a condensed outline of all aspects of Dutch grammar. It is a series of hints to help you use more effectively and with greater versatility phrases and vocabulary that you have already learned.

How to Study Essential Dutch Grammar

If you have already studied Dutch in a conventional manner, you can use this book as a refresher by glancing through all of it first and then selecting those areas on which you wish to concentrate.

If you have never studied Dutch grammar, then the following suggestions will be helpful:

1. Master several hundred useful phrases and expressions such as you will find in any good phrase book or in a recorded language course. You will understand the suggestions contained in *Essential Dutch Grammar* more easily after you have achieved this basic working knowledge of Dutch. The purpose of this book is to enable you to gain greater fluency once you have learned phrases and expressions, not to teach you to construct sentences from rules and vocabulary.

2. Read through *Essential Dutch Grammar* at least once in its entirety. Don't be concerned if anything is not immediately clear to you. What may appear discouragingly difficult at first will become easier as your studies progress. But the first reading is necessary to acquaint you with terms and concepts peculiar to Dutch grammar. Learning what these terms and concepts are will help you to improve your comprehension of Dutch and to use more freely the expressions you already know. As you use Dutch and hear it spoken, many of its grammatical patterns will become familiar to you. *Essential Dutch Grammar* helps you to discover these patterns so that you can use them.

3. Go back to this book periodically. Sections which seem difficult or of doubtful benefit at first may prove extremely useful later.

4. For the most part, the book follows a logical order, taking up the major divisions of grammar in sequence. You will do best to follow this order. However, some students learn best when they study to answer an immediate question or need (e.g., how to form the comparative; how to conjugate the verb "to be," etc.). If you are one of these students, turn to the section that interests you. But read through the entire section, rather than just an isolated part. Individual remarks, taken out of context, are easily misunderstood.

5. Examples are given for every rule. It is helpful to memorize these examples. If you learn every example in *Essential Dutch Grammar*, together with its literal translation, you will have encountered the basic difficulties of Dutch and studied models for their solution.

6. You cannot study Dutch systematically without an understanding of its grammar, and the use and understanding of grammatical terms is as essential as a knowledge of certain mechanical terms when you learn to drive a car. If your knowledge of grammatical terms is weak, read the Glossary of Grammatical Terms (p. 95) and refer to it whenever necessary.

In every language there are many ways to express the same thought. Some constructions are simple, others more difficult. During your first experiments in communication, use a simple construction. You may ultimately wish to master a more sophisticated way of expressing yourself. Be satisfied at first with the simplest.

As you begin to speak Dutch, you will become aware of the areas in which you need the most help in grammar. If you have no one with whom to speak, speak mentally to yourself. In the course of a day see how many of the simple thoughts you've expressed in English you are able to turn into Dutch. This kind of experimental self-testing will give direction to your study of grammar. Remember that you are studying this course in

Dutch not to pass an examination or to receive a certificate, but to communicate with others on a simple but useful level. *Essential Dutch Grammar* is not the equivalent of a formal course of study at a university. Although it could serve as a supplement to such a course, its primary aim is to help the adult study on his own. Indeed, no self-study or academic course or series of courses is ever ideally suited to all students. You must rely on and be guided by your own rate of learning and your own requirements and interests. *Essential Dutch Grammar* makes self-study easier.

If this or any other grammar tends to inhibit you in speaking Dutch or in using what you have learned through phrase books or conversation courses, curtail your study of grammar until you feel it will really assist rather than hinder your speaking. Your objective is speaking, and you *can* learn to speak a language without learning its grammar. But because of its systematic approach, grammar is a short-cut to language learning for those who feel at home with it. The fundamental purpose of *Essential Dutch Grammar* is to help you by eliminating hit-or-miss memorization.

SUGGESTIONS FOR VOCABULARY BUILDING

1. Study words and word lists that answer real and preferably immediate personal needs. If you are planning to travel in the near future, your motivation and orientation are clear-cut and a recorded language course or a good travel phrase book will provide you with the material you need. But select from this material that specifically applies to your case. For instance, if you don't plan to motor, don't spend time studying the parts of the car. If you like foreign foods, study the food lists in *Say It in Dutch*. Even if you do not plan to travel in the near future, you will probably learn more quickly by imagining a travel situation.

2. Memorize by association. Phrase books and recorded language courses usually give associated word lists. If you use a dictionary, don't memorize words haphazardly but choose words which are related and belong to the same family.

3. Study the specialized vocabulary of your profession, business, or hobby. If you are interested in real estate, learn the terms associated with property, buying, selling, leasing, etc. If you are interested in mathematics, acquire a vocabulary in this science. Many of these specialized words can be used in other areas too. You may not find specialized vocabularies in ordinary phrase books, but a good dictionary will help you to make up a list for your own use.

SPELLING

In order to learn Dutch grammar well, the student must first be familiar with the Dutch spelling system, since nouns, verbs, and adjectives often alter their spelling as endings are added. The reason for this is that, unlike English or French spelling, the written form of a Dutch word is a fairly faithful guide to its pronunciation. What initially may appear to the student as a bewildering and capricious change of spelling within a word is actually rigorous adherence to the principle that spelling must reflect pronunciation. To understand how the Dutch spelling system works the student must first recognize the difference between open and closed syllables and then learn five simple rules.

An *open syllable* is one that ends in a vowel (syllable breaks are shown in square brackets):

paling [pa-ling] (eel)	beter [be-ter] (better)
komen [ko-men] (to come)	meten [me-ten] (to measure)

A *closed syllable* is one that ends in a consonant:

les (lesson)	lessen [les-sen] (lessons)
paard (horse)	paarden [paar-den] (horses)
mens (human being)	mensen [men-sen] (human beings)

Regarding consonants occurring within a word, note that:

(1) a single consonant *begins* the following syllable: *hopen* [ho-pen] (to hope);

(2) two consonants are divided, the first one ending a syllable and the second one beginning the following syllable: *pudding* [pud-ding] (pudding), *feesten* [fees-ten] (festivals).

Rule I. A long vowel is represented by a double vowel letter in a closed syllable, and by a single vowel letter in an open syllable:

7

boom (tree)	long vowel, closed syllable
bomen [bo-men] (trees)	long vowel, open syllable
ik loop (I run)	long vowel, closed syllable
wij lopen [lo-pen] (we run)	long vowel, open syllable
rood (red)	long vowel, closed syllable
het rode [ro-de] licht (the red light)	long vowel, open syllable

Note that if a word ends on a long vowel, that vowel is spelled with a single letter. The exception to this rule is *ee*, which represents the long *e*-vowel at the end of a word:

ik ga (I go; from *gaan*, to go)
ik sla (I strike; from *slaan*, to strike)
nu (now)   vla (custard)   zo (so, thus)
BUT: twee (two)   zee (sea)   thee (tea)

Rule II.   Short vowels are always represented by a single letter and appear only in closed syllables. In other words, short vowels will be followed either by two consonants, or by one consonant at the end of a word:

smal (narrow)
de smalle [smal-le] weg (the narrow path)
pet (cap)   petten [pet-ten] (caps)
man (man)   mannen [man-nen] (men)

Note that the doubling of consonants in *petten* and *mannen* indicates visually that the vowel remains short in the plural (it is still contained within a closed syllable).

Note also that Rules I and II pertain only to the simple vowels *a, e, i, o, u*. They do not pertain to: (1) the diphthongs *au, ei, ij, ou, ui,* and *uw*; (2) vowels spelled with two different letters (*eu, ie, oe*); or (3) *aai, eeu, ieu, ooi,* or *oei*. Whether these sounds appear in open or closed syllables, their values and spelling remain the same.

Rule III.   No Dutch word may end on two identical consonants. In the Dutch spelling system a double consonant at the end of a word is redundant:

zitten (to sit)   ik zit (I sit)
bidden (to pray)   ik bid (I pray)
hebben (to have)   ik heb (I have)

Rule IV. The letters *f* and *s* change to *v* and *z*, respectively, when, owing to the addition of an ending, they begin rather than end a syllable:

brief (letter)	brieven [brie-ven] (letters)
lief (dear)	mijn lieve [lie-ve] moeder (my dear mother)
roos (rose)	rozen [ro-zen] (roses)
huis (house)	huizen [hui-zen] (houses)

Rule V (converse to Rule IV). The letters *v* and *z* change to *f* and *s*, respectively, when, owing to the change in the form of a word, they end rather than begin a syllable:

leven (to live)	Ik leef (I live)
	Ik leefde [leef-de] (I lived)
reizen (to travel)	Ik reis (I travel)
	Ik reisde [reis-de] (I traveled)

These rules for spelling will be repeated in the text at the appropriate places. The student is encouraged, however, to review this chapter before proceeding.

WORD ORDER

Dutch sentences employ three basic types of word order. The position of the working (conjugated) verb provides the focal point for their description. Once these three basic frameworks are familiar to the student, he will encounter few difficulties with Dutch sentence patterns.

Type I. In most Dutch sentences the working (conjugated) verb occupies *second position*. The subject of the sentence normally, but not always, takes first position. If some element other than the subject begins the sentence, the subject is regularly placed immediately after the working verb. Inactive verb forms (infinitives and past participles) come at the end of the sentence.

Sequence 1: subject, working verb (in italic), . . . , infinitive/participle

Ik *help* hem.	I help (am helping) him.
Hij *zal* ons helpen.	He will help us.
Het kind *wil* met de kat spelen.	The child wants to play with the cat.
Ik *heb* hem gisteren opgebeld.	I called him yesterday.
Ik *heb* hem vaak moeten helpen.	I often had to help him.

Sequence 2: first element (not the subject), working verb (in italic), subject, . . . , infinitive/participle

Wanneer *komt* hij terug?
When is he coming back?

Morgen *moeten* wij vertrekken.
We must leave tomorrow.

Met wie *hebt* u daarover gesproken?
With whom did you talk about it?

In de krant *heb* ik dat artikel gelezen.
It was in the newspaper that I read that article.

Deze man *wil* ik niet helpen.
I do not want to help this man.

Omdat het zo hard regent, *blijven* wij thuis.
Since it is raining so hard, we are staying home.

Note that almost any element may occupy first sentence position: question words, adverbs, prepositional phrases, object nouns and pronouns, or even an entire clause. Sentence elements with significant information value are often assigned first position, as are those ideas a speaker or writer wishes to emphasize.

Type II. In yes-and-no questions the working verb stands in first position, followed by the subject. The working verb also occupies first position in commands. If a subject is expressed, it follows the verb. Inactive verb forms (infinitives and past participles) occupy last position.

Sequence: working verb (in italic), subject, . . . , infinitive/participle

Zijn Piet en Ineke al thuis?
Are Piet and Ineke home already?

Leest u deze krant?
Do you read this newspaper?

Kun je hem morgen afhalen?
Can you pick him up tomorrow?

Kom toch mee!
Do come along!

Ga (jij) met hem mee!
(You) go along with him!

Heb je de nieuwe film al gezien?
Have you seen the new film already?

Type III. In dependent clauses the working verb comes at the *end of the clause.* Inactive verb forms generally precede the working verb, although they are sometimes placed after it. This is largely a question of usage and style and need not concern the beginning student. There are several kinds of dependent clauses and they will be treated individually in the appropriate chapters. For now the student should merely note the position of the italicized (working) verbs in the examples:

Ik zou graag weten waarom hij dat gedaan *heeft* (OR: *heeft* gedaan).
I would like to know why he did that.

Wij weten nog niet of hij ons morgen *opbellt*.
We do not know yet if he will call us tomorrow.

Hij zegt dat hij niet zingen *wil*.
He says that he does not want to sing.

Wij maken een wandeltocht, omdat het mooi weer *is*.
We are taking a walk because the weather is so nice.

Dat is de man, aan wie ik het boek *gaf*.
That is the man to whom I gave the book.

NEGATION

The question of negation is a complex one in any language. There are many subtle distinctions that may depend on the placement of a negative. The following rules, however, provide solid guidelines for negation in Dutch. Mastery of them will provide the beginning student with a working set of principles to cover most of the sentences he will encounter. In general, the English speaker should bear in mind that English tends to negate the verb itself in most instances: He speaks too loudly; he *doesn't* speak too loudly. This tendency will not be found in Dutch.

Rule I. In simple sentences the negative *niet* (not) comes last when the whole sentence is negated:

Ik weet het niet.	I don't know (it).
Hij ziet onze vrienden niet.	He doesn't see our friends.
Kom je of kom je niet?	Are you coming or aren't you?

Rule II. In sentences where a predicate adjective follows the verb "to be," *niet* immediately precedes the predicate adjective:

Ik ben niet rijk.	I am not wealthy.
Hij was niet dapper.	He was not brave.

Rule III. When *niet* negates one specific sentence element, it precedes that element:

Hij speelt niet goed.
He does not play well.

Hij heeft niet goed gespeeld.
He did not play well.

Dat doe ik niet graag.
I don't like to do that.
[LITERALLY: That I do not gladly].

13

Het zou niet lang duren als . . . .
It would not last long if . . . .

Hij gaat niet met de trein.
He is not going by train.

Ik wil er niet meer aan denken.
I don't want to think about it any more.

Zij zijn niet zo laat aangekomen.
They didn't arrive so (that) late.

Zo veel geld heb ik niet nodig.
I don't need that much money
[So much money have I not necessary].

In many sentences *niet* combines with an adjective or adverb to render one thought unit: *niet meer* (no longer), *nog niet* (not yet), *niet zo* (not so), *niet erg* (not very).

Rule IV. In sentences that end with an inactive verb form (infinitive or past participle) or a separable prefix, *niet* is generally placed immediately before them:

Ik had hem niet kunnen vinden.
I had not been able to find him.

Hij had zijn broodje niet opgegeten.
He had not eaten his sandwich.

Zij wil morgen niet komen.
She doesn't want to come tomorrow.

Het plan ging niet door.
The plan did not go through.

Rule V. In sentences in which one clause has Type III word order, *niet* is placed immediately before the verb form(s) at the end of that clause:

Ik weet dat hij niet komen wil.
I know that he doesn't want to come.

Ik weet dat Piet dat boek niet vertaald had.
I know that Piet had not translated that book.

Zijn zoon is tandarts, als ik me niet vergis.
His son is a dentist, if I am not mistaken.

Rule VI. Many English sentences negate the verb, while the equivalent Dutch sentence negates the direct object, using the adjective *geen* (no, not any):

Hij heeft geen geld.	He doesn't have any money (OR: He has no money).
Spreek je geen Nederlands?	Don't you speak any Dutch?

ARTICLES AND NOUNS

Indefinite Article

In English, the indefinite article is either "a" or "an." In Dutch the indefinite article has only one form, *een*:

    een man (a man)   een vrouw (a woman)
    een olifant (an elephant)

In informal speech and writing *een* is often reduced to *'n*. A stressed form of *een*, written *één*, means "one" as opposed to "more than one" or "several":

    één man (one man [not several])
    één hand (one hand [and no more])

Definite Articles

In English, the definite article has only one form, "the," but Dutch has two forms. All plural nouns take the form *de*. The situation is more complex for singular nouns. Dutch nouns are classified as being of either neuter or common gender, and the gender of a noun determines which of the two forms of the definite article is used with it in the *singular*. Neuter nouns take *het* in the singular, while *de* is used for common-gender nouns. Since gender in Dutch is largely a grammatical rather than a natural category, it is preferable to speak simply of *het*-words and *de*-words. Henceforth we will almost always use these terms rather than "neuter" and "common gender." In general, the student is best advised to learn each new Dutch noun together with its (singular) definite article, since there is no foolproof way for determining the gender of most nouns:

    de auto (the car)   het huis (the house)
    de vork (the fork)   het mes (the knife)

While memorizing the definite article as you learn each word is the best way of ensuring that you learn the gender of the word, there are nevertheless some general rules that can help you in recognizing and remembering the gender of a noun:

1. Nouns denoting male or female persons are most often *de*-words. Such nouns often show an agent suffix that marks them as *de*-words. Some of the more common suffixes are:

-aar	de leraar (the teacher)
	de Leidenaar (the citizen of Leiden)
-ent	de student (the student)
	de docent (the lecturer)
-er	de denker (the thinker)
	de danser (the dancer)
-es	de zangeres (the [female] singer
	de lerares (the [female] teacher)
-eur	de acteur (the actor)
	de directeur (the director)

2. All diminutives end in *-je* and are *het*-words even when they refer to persons:

het meisje (the girl)   het mannetje (the little man)
het kopje (the [small] cup)

3. Nouns that end in *-isme* are also *het*-words:

het communisme (communism)   het kapitalisme (capitalism)

4. All nouns ending in the following suffixes are *de*-words:

-heid	de godheid (the deity)
-ij	de slagerij (the butcher shop)
-ing	de herinnering (the memory)
-teit	de identiteit (the identity)
-tie	de kwestie (the question)

It should be noted that, in contrast to English, abstract nouns in Dutch are generally preceded by the definite article:

de moed (courage)   het leven (life)
het socialisme (socialism)

Noun Plurals

Dutch nouns are not inflected for case, but they do have plural forms in most instances. Most nouns form plurals in one of the two following ways:

1. The most common ending for the plural of nouns is *-en*:

het woord / de woorden	(the word / the words)
de hand / de handen	(the hand / the hands)
het huis / de huizen	(the house / the houses)
de kring / de kringen	(the circle / the circles)

Note that in addition to taking the *-en* ending, a few frequently occurring nouns also lengthen their root vowels in the plural. In the following words the vowels of the singular are short, while those of the plural are long:

de dag / de dagen	(the day / the days)
het glas / de glazen	(the glass / the glasses)
de slag / de slagen	(the blow / the blows)
het spel / de spelen	(the game / the games)
het slot / de sloten	(the castle / the castles)
de weg / de wegen	(the path / the paths)

At this point the student may want to return to pp. 7–8 to review the rules for long and short vowels.

2. The second most common plural ending is *-s*. Most nouns ending in unstressed *-aar*, *-aard*, *-el*, *-em*, *-en*, *-er*, as well as all diminutives, take *-s* in the plural:

de tafel / de tafels	(the table / the tables)
de bezem / de bezems	(the broom / the brooms)
de wagen / de wagens	(the car / the cars)
de kapper / de kappers	(the barber / the barbers)
het meisje / de meisjes	(the girl / the girls)
het huisje / de huisjes	(the small house / the small houses)

Note that the *-s* ending is also added to many words of foreign origin. The *-s* ending is preceded by an apostrophe if the word ends in *-a*, *-i*, *-o*, or *-u*:

de telefoon / de telefoons	(the telephone / the telephones)
de tante / de tantes	(the aunt / the aunts)

het drama / de drama's	(the drama / the dramas)
de ski / de ski's	(the ski / the skis)
de piano / de piano's	(the piano / the pianos)
de paraplu / de paraplu's	(the umbrella / the umbrellas)

In addition to the two most common ways of forming the plural there are three other plural endings that should be discussed. They do not apply to a great many nouns, but those to which they do apply occur frequently.

3. Several *het*-words form plurals by adding *-eren*. This ending is analogous to English *-ren* in "children":

het ei / de eieren	(the egg / the eggs)
het been / de beenderen	(the bone / the bones; note the added *-d-*)
het blad / de bladeren	(the leaf / the leaves)
het kind / de kinderen	(the child / the children)
het lied / de liederen	(the song / the songs)

4. A few commonly occurring nouns undergo a change of their root vowels in forming the plural. They also take the ending *-en*:

het lid / de leden	(the member, limb / the members, limbs)
het schip / de schepen	(the ship / the ships)
de smid / de smeden	(the blacksmith / the blacksmiths)
de stad / de steden	(the city / the cities)

5. Words from Latin that end in *-us* generally form their plural in *-i* if they refer to persons:

de musicus / de musici	(the musician / the musicians)

They are given a Dutch plural, however, if they refer to objects or things:

de cursus / de cursussen	(the course / the courses)

Nouns from the Latin that end in *-um* replace *-um* either with the Latin plural *-a* or the Dutch plural *-s*:

het museum / de musea OR de museums	(the museum / the museums)

6. Dutch nouns that indicate measure or quantity do not take a plural ending:

> honderd kilometer (a hundred kilometers)
> vijf jaar (five years)
> tien meter (ten meters)

Diminutives: Form and Function

The frequent use of diminutives is a characteristic of the Dutch language. They are a much more important feature in Dutch than they are in English or German, and it is no exaggeration to say that one cannot really speak Dutch without a feeling for its use of diminutives. Diminutives often indicate smallness, but they may also express a variety of attitudes toward an object or person: familiarity, affection, tenderness, irony, or even disdain. Often they lend an untranslatable connotation to a word, something that only the native speaker can perceive. Diminutives are always *het*-words and always take *-s* in the plural. To form a diminutive most nouns add the suffix *-je*:

> de voet / het voetje   (the foot / the [cute] little foot)
> het huis / het huisje   (the house / the [cozy] little house)
> het dorp / het dorpje   (the village / the tiny [and perhaps remote] village)

The diminutive suffix may appear in several variations of *-je*, the most important of which are:

> *-tje*   de stoel / het stoeltje   (the chair / the small chair)
> *-etje* de bal / het balletje   (the ball / the tiny ball)
> *-pje*   de arm / het armpje   (the arm / the [dainty] little arm)

Remember that the addition of a diminutive suffix changes *de*-class nouns to *het*-class.

Adjectives as Nouns

Adjectives may also function as nouns when the qualities they describe are attributed to persons or things that themselves are unexpressed. In such cases the adjective is preceded by an article, definite or indefinite, and takes the ending *-e* in the singular and *-en* in the plural:

een rijke (a wealthy [person])
de rijke (the wealthy [person])
de rijken (the wealthy [persons])
het mooie (the beautiful [thing, aspect])

Infinitives as Nouns

Dutch may employ an infinitive form to function as a noun, corresponding to what in English is called a *gerund* (the verbal noun, ending in " -ing "). An infinitive so used may, but need not, be preceded by the article *het* (Dutch has no separate verb form that is exactly like the English gerund):

Hij schudde van het *lachen* (infinitive).
He shook from *laughing* (gerund).

Ik ging door met *zingen* (infinitive).
I continued *singing* (gerund).

ADJECTIVES

Adjective Endings

The only common adjective ending in modern Dutch is *-e* (*-s* is used infrequently). Endings are applied to adjectives in the following cases:

1. Before all plural nouns:

hoge dijken (high dikes)   snelle treinen (fast trains)

2. After the definite articles *de* and *het* and the demonstrative adjectives (see p. 34):

de lange muur (the long wall)
het lage land (the low land)

deze zonnige straat (this sunny street)
dit nieuwe huis (this new house)

3. After the indefinite article *een* (or *geen*, "no, not any") when the noun modified is a *de*-word:

de dag (the day)   een lange dag (a long day)
de melk (the milk)   geen warme melk (no warm milk)

4. After the pronouns *iets* (something), *niets* (nothing), *veel* (much), *wat* (something) and *weinig* (little), adjectives take the ending *-s*:

iets moois (something beautiful)   niets nieuws (nothing new)
weinig goeds (little that is good)

The adjective remains without an ending in the following cases:

1. When it does not precede the noun it modifies, that is, when it functions as a predicate adjective:

Het weer is warm.   The weather is warm.
BUT: het warme weer   the warm weather

22

De wijn is rood.   The wine is red.
BUT: de rode wijn   the red wine

2. When in the singular it modifies an *het*-word and is preceded by *een, geen, elk* (each), *ieder* (each), *menig* (many a), *veel* (much), *welk* (which), or *zo'n* (such a):

    het huis (the house)   een oud huis (an old house)
    het kopje (the cup)   een duur kopje (an expensive cup)
    het paard (the horse)   welk oud paard (which old horse)

3. When in the singular it modifies an *het*-word and is not itself preceded by any qualifier:

    het brood (the bread)   vers brood (fresh bread)
    het water (the water)   heet water (hot water)

4. When in modifying a (usually male) person it characterizes the personal or professional stature or the innate qualities of that person and is preceded by *een*:

    een beroemd kunstenaar (a famous artist)
    een verstandig leraar (a wise teacher)

5. Adjectives ending in -*en* remain uninflected regardless of their position:

    de houten trap (the wooden staircase)
    wollen sokken (woollen socks)

6. The adjectives for "left" and "right," and adjectives derived from place names and ending in -*er*, also remain uninflected:

    mijn linker hand (my left hand)
    zijn rechter oog (his right eye)
    een Edammer kaas (an Edam cheese)
    Deventer koekjes (Deventer cookies)

In literary or idiomatic usage exceptions to the above rules occur, but the rules stated cover the vast majority of situations. In literary usage one encounters from time to time certain fixed expressions that show adjective and noun endings no longer active in modern Dutch. Thus: *van koninklijken bloede* (of royal blood), *van ganser harte* (from the bottom of one's heart). These and similar petrified forms point to a stage in the history of

Dutch when it was a much more highly inflected language. Dutch, like English, has in the course of its development discarded many inflectional endings.

Present Participles as Adjectives

In English the present participle is formed by adding " -ing " to the verb. It then may function as an adjective: " the laughing cow," " the singing sisters." The present participle is a verbal adjective: it is verbal in that it expresses activity (singing, dancing, smiling, etc.) and it is an adjective because it can describe or qualify a noun. To form the present participle in Dutch, simply add a -d to the verb infinitive (see p. 45). The participle is then inflected according to the rules for adjectives:

de lachende koe (the laughing cow)
de volgende week (the following week)
de zingende zusters (the singing sisters)
een schreiend kind (a crying child)
schreiende kinderen (crying children)

Past Participles as Adjectives

Past participles may also function as adjectives in Dutch, much as they do in English. The formation of the past participle is discussed in detail in the chapter on verbs (pp. 51–53). For now it will suffice to note that some past participles end in -en, others in -d (-t). Those ending in -en (like adjectives ending in -en) do not add an inflectional ending when used as adjectives, while those ending in -d (-t) are inflected according to the normal rules for adjectives:

de gesloten deur (the closed door)
de gesloten deuren (the closed doors)
een verwend kind (a spoiled child)
verwende kinderen (spoiled children)
een gereserveerde kamer (a reserved room)
gereserveerde kamers (reserved rooms)
zijn gedrukte werken (his published works)

Like the present participle, the past participle combines the functions of adjective and verb. Unlike the present participle, however, the activity expressed in the past participle is one performed *upon* the noun modified. The present participle describes activity that the modified noun is itself performing. Note the distinction:

de zingende zusters (the singing sisters, i.e., the sisters who are singing)

geslepen diamanten (polished diamonds, i.e., diamonds that have been polished)

In other words, the present participle is *active* in meaning, and the past participle *passive.*

Comparison

English regularly employs one of two methods to form comparative adjectives. Either an "-er" and "-est" are added to form the comparative and superlative, respectively ("long, longer, longest"), or "more" and "most" express the degrees of comparison ("brilliant, more brilliant, most brilliant"). The former system is common to all the Germanic languages; English has taken over the latter from the Romance languages. In general, the Dutch system coincides with that of the other Germanic languages. Only occasionally, for reasons of pronunciation, does Dutch add *meest* (most) to form the superlative of an adjective.

The **comparative degree** of adjectives is regularly formed by adding *-er*. The adjective is then inflected according to the general rules already outlined:

jong (young)   jonger (younger)
een jonge man (a young man)
een jong meisje (a young girl)
een jongere man (a younger man)
een jonger meisje (a younger girl)
de jongere man (the younger man)
het jongere meisje (the younger girl)
Het meisje is jonger dan de man.
The girl is younger than the man.

Adjectives that end in *-r* insert a *-d-* before the comparative suffix:

dapper (brave)   dapper*d*er (braver)
duur (expensive)   duur*d*er (more expensive)

lekker (tasty)	lekkerder (tastier)
ver (far)	verder (farther, further)
zwaar (heavy)	zwaarder (heavier)

If the comparative form of the adjective has three or more syllables, no inflectional ending is added:

eenvoudig (simple)
een eenvoudiger oplossing (a simpler solution)
gemakkelijk (comfortable)
een gemakkelijker stoel (a more comfortable chair)

The **superlative degree** of most adjectives is formed by adding -*st* (-*t* if the adjective ends in -*s*) to the basic adjective. It too is then inflected like a simple adjective:

oud (old)   oudst (oldest)
een oude man (an old man)
een oud schip (an old ship)
de oudste man (the oldest man)
het oudste schip (the oldest ship)

vers (fresh)   verst (freshest)
de verse boter (the fresh butter)
het verse vlees (the fresh meat)
de verste boter (the freshest butter)
het verste vlees (the freshest meat)

When, however, the superlative adjective is a predicate adjective (that is, when it follows the verb "to be" and does not precede a noun), it must be preceded by *het*:

Die handtas is het mooist(e).	That handbag is the most beautiful.
Dit boek is het best(e).	This book is (the) best.

The -*e* ending on *mooiste* and *beste* in the sentences above is optional, and since its use is largely a question of sentence rhythm, it need not concern the beginning student.

In contrast to English, Dutch uses the superlative to compare two or more things:

Zij is de jongste van de twee zusters.
She is the younger of the two sisters.

Zij is de jongste van de drie zusters.
She is the youngest of the three sisters.

The following adjectives have **irregular** comparatives:

goed (good)	beter (better)	best (best)
veel (much)	meer (more)	meest (most)
weinig (little)	minder (less)	minst (least)

Note also: "Than" is *dan* in comparisons:

De man is ouder dan de vrouw.
The man is older than the woman.

"As . . . as" is *zo* (OR: *even*) . . . *als*:

De vrouw is zo (OR: even) oud als de man.
The woman is as old as the man.

Ordinal Numbers

For most of the numbers from one to nineteen, ordinal numbers ("first," "second," etc.) are formed by adding -*de* to the cardinal number:

twee (two)   tweede (second)   vier (four)   vierde (fourth)

Irregular ordinals are *eerst* (first), *derde* (third), and *achtste* (eighth). All ordinals beyond nineteen are formed by adding -*ste* to the cardinal number:

drieëntwintig (twenty-three)   drieëntwintigste (twenty-third)
zeventig (seventy)   zeventigste (seventieth)

With nouns, ordinal numbers are used like other adjectives. The only one that declines is *eerst*, however, since all the others already end in -*e*. In writing, the ordinals are often represented in abbreviated form, as *1e, 2e, 3e*, etc., or *1ste, 2de, 3de*, etc.

ADVERBS

In English, adverbs are usually formed by adding "-ly" to adjectives: sweet, sweet*ly*; serious, serious*ly*. Adverbs in Dutch take no inflectional endings and change their basic form only in the comparative and superlative degrees. By and large, Dutch adverbs are identical in form to the uninflected adjectives from which they are derived:

vroeg (early)	Hij staat vroeg op.	He gets up early.
goed (good)	Zij zingt goed.	She sings well.
lang (long)	Het duurde te lang.	It lasted too long.

Like English, Dutch of course has a number of adverbs for which there is no adjectival equivalent: *ooit* (ever), *nooit* (never), *nu* (now), *erg* (very), *weer* (again), *altijd* (always), and several others. This type of adverb is absolute in meaning and thus does not have a comparative or superlative degree.

Comparison

Adverbs form the **comparative degree** in the same way as adjectives: they simply add the suffix *-er* to the basic form. As is the case with adjectives, adverbs ending in *-r* insert a *d* before adding *-er*: *duur* (expensive, expensively); *duurder* (more expensive, more expensively).

snel (fast, quick)	Hij loopt sneller dan ik.
	He runs faster than I.
ver (far)	Zij willen verder gaan.
	They want to go further.
langzaam (slow)	U moet langzamer praten.
	You must speak more slowly.

The **superlative degree** of adverbs is formed by adding the suffix *-st(e)*. The superlative is always preceded by *het*. The optional *-e* ending of the superlative is largely a question of sentence rhythm and need not concern the beginning student:

mooi (beautiful)	Zij zong het mooist(e).
	She sang most beautifully.
vlug (fast, quick)	Hij leert het vlugst(e).
	He learns the most quickly.
lang (long)	Eerlijk duurt het langst.
	Honesty is the best policy.
	[LITERALLY: Honestly lasts the longest.]

Irregular Adverbs

In the preceding chapter it was noted that a few adjectives have irregular comparatives. The most commonly occurring irregular adjectives are:

goed (good)	beter (better)	best (best)
veel (much)	meer (more)	meest (most)
weinig (little)	minder (less)	minst (least)

The equivalent adverbs have the same irregularities and differ from the adjectives in that they must be preceded by *het* in the superlative.

To these might be added two adverbs that also show irregular comparisons:

| na (near) | nader (nearer) | het naast(e) (nearest) |
| dikwijls (often) | vaker (more often) | het vaakst (most often) |

The adverb *dikwijls* (often) has no comparative and superlative forms of its own and thus borrows them from the adverb *vaak*, which also means "often."

The Adverb *Graag*

The adverb *graag* (gladly, willingly) has the irregular comparative *liever* (more gladly, more willingly) and superlative *het liefst* (most gladly, most willingly). Note carefully how the following sentences translate into English:

Ik kijk graag naar de TV.	I like to watch TV.
Zij gaat liever dansen.	She prefers to go dancing.
Hij leest het liefst een boek.	He likes best of all to read a book.

Notice that in English the idea of liking or having a preference tends to be expressed in the verb ("like," "prefer"), while in Dutch the various forms of the adverb *graag* express this idea.

Adverbs of Time

The names of the parts of the day and the weekdays function adverbially in the following expressions:

's morgens [OR: 's ochtends]	(in the morning)
s' avonds	(in the evening)
's middags	(in the afternoon)
's nachts	(at night)
zondags [OR: 's zondags]	(Sundays)
maandags [OR: 's maandags]	(Mondays)
dinsdags	(Tuesdays)
woensdags [OR: 's woensdags]	(Wednesdays)
donderdags	(Thursdays)
vrijdags	(Fridays)
zaterdags	(Saturdays)

These adverbs are derived from old genitive case forms of the nouns. They indicate repeated, habitual action.

"Where"

In current standard English, speakers and writers do not distinguish between "where" (at what place) and "where" (to what place; in older English, "whither"):

Where is he (at) now?   Where is he going (to)?

In contrast, Dutch uses the adverb *waar* only in the sense of "at what place." For "where" meaning "to what place" Dutch uses either *waar . . . naar toe* or *waarheen*:

Waar wonen zij?	Where do they live?
Waar gaat hij naar toe?	Where is he going?
Waarheen gaat hij?	Where is he going?

English and Dutch usage coincide in specifying where someone or something is coming from:

Waar komt hij vandaan?   Where is he coming from?

Word Order: Time, Manner, Place

When several adverbs or adverbial phrases occur in a sentence, they tend to be arranged in the order: time, manner, place (in contrast to Dutch, English prefers place elements before time elements):

Hij gaat morgen [time] met zijn vrouw [manner] naar Leiden [place].
He is going to Leiden tomorrow with his wife.

Since adverbs frequently begin Dutch sentences, this sentence might also be phrased as follows:

Morgen gaat hij met zijn vrouw naar Leiden.

Note also:

Ik ging gisteren [time] met de trein [manner] naar Amsterdam [place].
OR: Gisteren ging ik met de trein naar Amsterdam.
I went by train to Amsterdam yesterday.

POSSESSIVES AND POSSESSION

Dutch possessives may function as either adjectives or pronouns—adjectives ("my," "your") if they modify a noun, pronouns ("mine," "yours") if they replace a noun. For either situation the basic forms can be seen in the following table. The unstressed forms given in parentheses are allowable forms that occur only when the possessive functions as an adjective:

mijn (m'n)	my OR mine
jouw (je)	your OR yours (SINGULAR FAMILIAR)
zijn (z'n)	his, its
haar (d'r)	her OR hers
uw	your OR yours (POLITE)
ons / onze	our OR ours
jullie (je)	your OR yours (PLURAL FAMILIAR)
hun (d'r)	their OR theirs

1. When possessives function as **adjectives**, they simply come before the noun they modify. They do not take endings or change their form. The only exception is "our": *ons* comes before singular nouns of the *het*-class, *onze* before all other nouns.

mijn auto('s)	my car(s)
zijn vriend(en)	his friend(s)
haar ring(en)	her ring(s)
jouw moeder	your mother
ons huis	our house
onze huizen	our houses
onze leraar(s)	our teacher(s)
jullie vader	your father

Unstressed forms are common in relaxed, informal speech and writing: *m'n auto* (my car), *z'n vriend* (his friend), *je moeder* (your mother).

2. When possessives function as **pronouns**, they are preceded by the appropriate definite article and add the ending *-e* to the stressed form (*jullie* is the only one of the possessives that cannot be used in this construction; see the next paragraph):

het boek	(the book)	het mijne	(mine [i.e., my book])
het kopje	(the cup)	het zijne	(his [i.e., his cup])
de fiets	(the bicycle)	de hare	(hers [her bicycle])
de auto	(the car)	de hunne	(theirs [their car])

Zijn werk is beter dan het mijne.	His work is better than mine.
Welke fiets is de onze?	Which bicycle is ours?
Welk kind is het jouwe?	Which child is yours?

In many sentences in which the verb "to be" occurs, the idea of possession is expressed through the preposition *van* (by, from, of) and the object form of the personal pronoun (see the chapter on pronouns for these forms). In the case of *jullie* this is the only way to indicate possession:

Is deze pen van jou?	Is this pen yours?
Die schoenen zijn niet van mij.	Those shoes are not mine.
Zijn deze brieven van jullie?	Are these letters yours?
Die van jullie zijn groot.	Yours are large [LITERALLY: Those of you are large].

Relationships of possession between nouns are normally expressed in Dutch in a form corresponding to English "the friend of the doctor" (*van* = of) rather than to English "the doctor's friend":

| de vriend van de dokter | the doctor's friend |
| de kat van het meisje | the girl's cat |

In informal speech and writing, another construction is often used:

Loek z'n vader
Luke's father [Luke his father]
INSTEAD OF : de vader van Loek

mijn vriend z'n broer
my friend's brother [my friend his brother]
INSTEAD OF : de broer van mijn vriend

haar zuster d'r huis
her sister's house [her sister her house]
INSTEAD OF : het huis van haar zuster

DEMONSTRATIVE ADJECTIVES
AND PRONOUNS

Demonstrative **adjectives** in Dutch agree with the nouns they modify in number and gender. They have the following forms:

het-WORDS	*de*-WORDS	
dit	deze	this
deze	deze	these
dat	die	that
die	die	those

dit bord (this plate)	deze trein (this train)
deze borden (these plates)	deze treinen (these trains)
dat bord (that plate)	die trein (that train)
die borden (those plates)	die treinen (those trains)

As in English, the demonstrative **pronouns** in Dutch have the same forms as the demonstrative adjectives. Instead of modifying a noun, however, they take its place when the noun is understood and can thus be omitted. The demonstrative pronoun has the same gender and number that the missing noun would have.

Dit huis is mooier dan *dat*.
This house is more beautiful than that (one).

Deze boeken zijn duurder dan *die*.
These books are more expensive than those.

Hij sprak niet over die vrouw maar over *deze*.
He was not talking about that woman but about this one.

The demonstratives *dit* and *dat* are used when the pronouns are unspecified (not relating to a specific understood noun), whether the object pointed out is singular or plural:

Wat is dat?	What is that?
Dat is een horloge.	That is a watch.

34

Dat zijn horloges.	Those are watches.
Wat is dit?	What is this?
Dit is een tijdschrift.	This is a magazine.
Dit zijn tijdschriften.	These are magazines.

PRONOUNS

Personal Pronouns

The personal pronouns in Dutch have differing stressed and unstressed forms as well as subject and object forms. The following table lists all the personal pronouns with their unstressed forms in parentheses:

	SUBJECT FORM		OBJECT FORM
	SINGULAR		
I	ik ('k)	me	mij (me)
you (FAMILIAR)	jij (je)	you (FAMILIAR)	jou (je)
he	hij (ie)	him	hem ('m)
she	zij (ze)	her	haar (d'r / 'r)
it	het ('t)	it	het ('t)
you (POLITE)	u	you (POLITE)	u
	PLURAL		
we	wij (we)	us	ons
you (FAMILIAR)	jullie (je)	you (FAMILIAR)	jullie (je)
they	zij (ze)	them	hun / hen (ze)
you (POLITE)	u	you (POLITE)	u

1. The unstressed forms in parentheses are commonly used in the spoken language when the speaker does not wish to place any particular emphasis on the pronoun. Speakers of English also tend to use unstressed forms of the pronoun. In English, however, we generally write the full form of the pronoun: "I saw them" rather than "I saw 'em." Of the unstressed forms in Dutch, *me, je, ze, 't*, and *we* are also quite common in the written language. This text generally uses the stressed forms of the personal pronouns.

2. Note that there are three separate pronouns for "you": a singular familiar form *jij*, a plural familiar form *jullie*, and a polite form *u* that is used for both singular and plural. In general, the Dutch use the familiar forms with family members, close friends, and children, making a distinction between singular and plural. With strangers, superiors, and superficial or business acquaintances the *u*-form is used. It expresses respect and deference. The *u*-form always requires a singular verb, regardless of how many people are being addressed. Note also that the polite *u*-form has the same subject and object forms, as does the plural familiar form *jullie*.

3. There are two stressed object forms for "them": *hun* and *hen*. Strictly speaking, Dutch maintains a distinction between the indirect object form *hun* and the direct object and prepositional object form *hen*. In practice, however, most Dutch speakers and writers prefer *hun* in both cases, or they replace both forms with the unstressed *ze*. *Ze* is always used when referring to inanimate objects.

4. The personal pronouns for the third person singular also require some comment. When referring to males or male animals, the Dutch use *hij*. For females or female animals the pronoun is *zij*. If an inanimate object belongs to the *het*-class of nouns, it is referred to with the pronoun *het*: *Het huis is mooi. Het is mooi.* (The house is beautiful. It is beautiful.) Many inanimate objects belong to the *de*-class of nouns, however, and thus the question arises which pronoun should be used when referring to them. In general, Dutch chooses *hij* (English, in contrast, almost always refers to inanimate objects as "it"):

De pen is nieuw. *Hij* is nieuw. The pen is new. *It* is new.
Mijn fiets is oud. *Hij* is oud. My bicycle is old. *It* is old.

5. In regard to subject and object forms English and Dutch usage is essentially the same:

Ik zie haar. I see her.
Zij ziet mij. She sees me.
Wij gaan met hem. We are going with him.
Hij gaat met ons. He is going with us.
Ik geef hem de brief. I am giving him the letter.
Ik geef de brief aan hem. I am giving the letter to him.

In both English and Dutch, direct and indirect objects and objects of prepositions require the object form of the pronoun, while subjects require the subject form.

The Word *Er* and Pronoun Substitutes

Prepositions in Dutch do not take a personal pronoun object if the pronoun refers to an inanimate object. There is thus nothing in Dutch comparable to the English "with it," "against it," "for it," and the like. Instead, Dutch prefixes the word *er* to the preposition in place of the pronoun:

*er*op (on it)   *er*voor (for it)   *er*over (over it, about it)

Ten slotte is hij *erin* geslaagd.	Finally he succeeded *at it.*
Wij hebben hem *ervoor* gedankt.	We thanked him *for it.*
Ik vraag hem *erom.*	I am asking him *for it.*

This construction corresponds to English words of the type "therewith," "thereupon," "thereof."

It is quite common in Dutch to separate *er* from its preposition. Frequently an adverb or an object comes between the two words:

Ben je *er* zeker *van?*
Are you certain *of it?*

Ik wacht *er* al lang *op.*
I have been waiting a long time *for it.*

Wij hebben *er* veel last *van.*
We have much trouble *from it* (*with it*).

For emphasis *er* is often replaced by *daar* (there) or *hier* (here). These may also be separated from their prepositions:

Daarvan heb ik niets gehoord (OR: *Daar* heb ik niets *van* gehoord).
I have heard nothing *about that.*

When the prepositions *met* (with) and *tot* (to) appear in this construction, they change their form to *mee* and *toe*, respectively:

Het kind speelt *ermee.*
The child is playing *with it.*

Daar wil ik niets *mee* te doen hebben.
With that I will have nothing to do.

Ik besluit *hiermee* mijn verhaal.
I conclude *herewith* my tale.

Hoe bent u *daartoe* gekomen?
How did you come *to* (do) *it*?

The word er has a number of other uses. Note the following:

1. *Er* is the equivalent of English " there " in sentences of the type " There is . . . " or " There are . . . " referring to the existence of a thing rather than its location:

Er is nog tijd om . . . .
There is still time to . . . .

Er zijn veel mensen in deze stad.
There are many people in this city.

2. But in other situations *er* can mean " there " when referring to place:

Ik woon er niet meer.   I no longer live there.

3. *Er* may also have the partitive meaning " of it," "of them ":

Ik heb er maar drie.   I only have three of them.

Reflexive Pronouns

When the subject of a sentence acts upon itself, the object is expressed as a reflexive pronoun. Note the following. " I see *myself* in the mirror," " They wash *themselves* every day." The reflexive pronoun occurs most frequently as a direct object, but may also function as an indirect object: " He buys *himself* (IND. OBJ.) a new car (DIR. OBJ.)," " She bought *herself* (IND. OBJ.) a hat (DIR. OBJ.)." The main idea with reflexive pronouns is that subject and object be the same person, that the object pronoun " reflect " the subject.

Reflexive pronouns in Dutch correspond with the object form of the personal pronoun for the first and second persons, singular and plural: *mij* (*me*), *jou* (*je*), *ons*, *jullie* (*je*). For the third person singular and plural, however, the form *zich* is used. For the polite *u*-form either *zich* or *u* may occur:

Ik was me.   I wash (myself). I get washed.
Jij wast je.   You wash (yourself). You get washed.
Hij (zij) wast zich.   He (she) washes (himself/herself).
                           He (she) gets washed.

U wast zich (u).	You wash (yourself). You get washed.
Wij wassen ons.	We wash (ourselves). We get washed.
Jullie wassen je.	You wash (yourselves). You get washed.
Zij wassen zich.	They wash (themselves). They get washed.

The use of reflexive pronouns is much more widespread in Dutch than in English. Dutch has many reflexive constructions which have only nonreflexive equivalents in English:

Ik *voel me* goed.	I *feel* well.
Jij moet *je haasten.*	You must *hurry.*
Hij *kleedt zich* goed.	He *dresses* well.
Wij *vergissen ons.*	We *make a mistake.*
Zij *verbazen zich.*	They *are surprised.*
Ik *verheug me* erop.	I *am looking forward* to it.
Herinner je (SUBJ.) *je*	Do *you remember* that man?
(IND. OBJ.) die man?	
Wij *vervelen ons.*	We *are bored.*
Ik *stel me* (IND. OBJ.) iets	I *imagine* something.
(DIR. OBJ.) *voor.*	

The word *zelf* (self) may have one of two functions:

1. When added as a suffix to a reflexive pronoun, it lends it emphasis:

Hij wast zichzelf.
He washes himself (no one else washes him).

2. As an intensive pronoun it may add emphasis to the subject noun or pronoun:

Hij heeft het zelf gedaan.
He did it himself (no one helped him).

The English pronouns "each other" and "one another" indicate mutual action carried out by a plural subject. These pronouns are called *reciprocal* pronouns and their most common equivalent in Dutch is *elkaar*:

Wij hebben elkaar vaak gezien.
We often saw each other.

Zij hebben elkaar altijd geholpen.
They always helped one another.

The Indefinite Pronoun *Men*

The indefinite pronoun *men* may be translated into English as "one," "they," "you," "people," or sometimes with a passive construction. The main idea is that of action performed by an unspecified agent or agents. The focus of attention is the activity and not the agent, and so the agent need not be identified. *Men* always requires a verb in the third person singular:

Men zegt dat zij een grote zangeres is.
They say she is a great singer.

Men heeft hem erg bewonderd.
He was greatly admired.

Men moet dieven met dieven vangen.
It takes a thief to catch a thief
[One must catch thieves with thieves].

In the spoken language it is more common to use *je* (you) or *ze* (they) as the subject of this type of sentence. In this respect, Dutch and English usage are quite similar:

Ze zeggen dat het mooi weer blijft.
They say the weather will stay nice.

Je kunt nooit weten of . . . .
You can never tell (know) if . . . .

Je kunt daarover lachen.
You can laugh about it.

As in English, Dutch has no specific "you" or "they" in mind in such statements.

Interrogatives

The interrogative **pronouns** in Dutch are *wie* (who[m], which) and *wat* (what). Neither word has a separate object form:

Wie/Wat is dat?
Who/What is that?

Wat/Wie heb je gezien?
What/Whom did you see?

Aan wie heb je de brief geschreven?
To whom did you write the letter?

Met wie ga je naar Amsterdam?
With whom are you going to Amsterdam?

Wie van jullie kan ons helpen?
Which of you can help us?

Interrogative "whose" may be expressed in two ways: *van wie* and *wie z'n*, the latter being confined to the spoken language:

Van wie is deze auto?
Whose car is this? [Of whom is this car?]

Van wie zijn die handschoenen?
Whose gloves are those?

Wie z'n hoed is dat?
Whose hat is that?

Wie z'n ring ligt op de tafel?
Whose ring is lying on the table?

The interrogative **adjectives** "which, what" are rendered in Dutch by *welk(e)*, *welk* being used with singular nouns of the *het*-class and *welke* with all other nouns:

Welk huis is het mooiste?
Which house is the most beautiful?

Welke man / vrouw bedoel je?
Which man / woman do you mean?

Welke appels wil je kopen?
Which apples do you want to buy?

"What sort of" is rendered in Dutch by *wat voor* (OR *wat voor een*):

Wat voor een leraar is hij?
What sort of a teacher is he?

Wat voor romans hebben zij gelezen?
What sort of novels did they read?

Relative Pronouns

1. The relative pronoun has two basic forms in Dutch. They are *die* (who[m], that) and *dat* (that, which), the former for all *de*-class noun antecedents and all plurals, the latter for singular antecedents of the *het*-class. The relative pronoun has no separate object form, the same form being used for subject and object. The clause introduced by a relative pronoun requires Type III word order (see p. 11):

> Hij is de man die ik uitgenodigd had.
> He is the man (whom) I had invited.

> Hij is de man die mij uitgenodigd had.
> He is the man who had invited me.

> Dat is de vrouw die ik bedoel.
> That is the woman (that) I mean.

> Dat is het boek dat pas verschenen is.
> That is the book that has just appeared.

> Dat is het boek dat ik las.
> That is the book (that) I read.

Note that, unlike English, Dutch never omits the relative pronoun.

2. The pronoun *wie* replaces *die* when the relative pronoun follows a preposition:

> De jongen met wie ik praatte heet Piet.
> The boy with whom I spoke is called Piet.

> De vrouw van wie ik gehoord heb . . . .
> The woman about whom I heard . . . .

> Is dat niet de man over wie hij gesproken heeft?
> Isn't that the man about whom he was speaking?

3. Prepositional compounds with *waar*- may replace the combination of preposition-plus-relative-pronoun when referring to persons, and **must** replace this combination when referring to inanimate objects. *Waar* is often separated from its preposition:

> Dat zijn mensen *waarop* je rekenen kunt.
> They (Those) are people *upon whom* you can count
> (OR: people you can count on).

> Hij is een jongen *waar* men zich *aan* ergert.
> He is a boy *with whom* you get annoyed
> (a boy you get annoyed with).

De jongen *waarmee* ik praatte heet Arie.
The boy *with whom* I was talking is called Arie.

De bal *waarmee* hij speelde . . . .
The ball *with which* he was playing . . . .

4. The pronoun "whoever," a relative pronoun without a specific antecedent, is rendered in Dutch by *wie*:

Wie zo leeft, leeft eerlijk.
Whoever lives this way, lives honorably.

Wie er over nadenkt, ziet in dat . . . .
Whoever thinks about it, realizes that . . . .

5. The pronoun *wat* is used in place of *dat* when the relative pronoun refers back to the words *alles* (everything), *iets* (something), *niets* (nothing); or to the superlative form of an adjective used as a noun; or to the whole preceding clause. It is also used when there is no specific antecedent (corresponding to English "what" rather than to "that" or "which"):

Dat is alles wat ik heb.
That is everything that I have.

Het hoogste wat wij bereiken kunnen . . . .
The best (highest) that we can attain . . . .

Hij komt altijd te laat, wat ons ergert.
He always comes too late, which annoys us.

Als zij morgen komen, wat ik betwijfel . . . .
If they come tomorrow, which I doubt . . . .

Hij zegt altijd wat hij bedoelt.
He always says what he means.

VERBS

The Present Tense

The present tense of verbs is formed by adding the appropriate personal endings to the stem of the verb. To find the stem of a verb simply drop its infinitive -*en* (or, rarely, -*n*) ending. The stem of the verb *zingen* (to sing) is thus *zing-*, for the verb *doen* (to do) it is *doe-*. It should be noted that verbs are always listed in dictionaries and grammars under their infinitive form. The endings for the present tense are: -*t* for the second and third persons singular and for the *u*-form, and -*en* for all plural forms. The first person singular coincides with the stem form of the verb:

ik	zing	doe	I sing, do
jij	zingt	doet	you sing, do
hij	zingt	doet	he sings, does
u	zingt	doet	you sing, do
wij	zingen	doen	we sing, do
jullie	zingen	doen	you sing, do
zij	zingen	doen	they sing, do

In accordance with the general rules for spelling (see that section), the following spelling changes must be made when writing verb stems:

1. When the stem vowel of an infinitive is long and in an open syllable, that vowel must be doubled when the infinitive ending is removed: *maken* (to make) has the stem *maak-*, *horen* (to hear) has the stem *hoor-*. When the plural endings in -*en* are added to the stem, it again becomes an open syllable and thus is written with just one vowel: *ik maak* (I make) but *wij maken* (we make), *ik hoor* (I hear) but *wij horen* (we hear).

2. When an infinitive has a short stem vowel followed by a double consonant, one of the consonants is dropped in spelling

45

the stem: *zitten* (to sit) has the stem *zit-*, *leggen* (to lay) has the stem *leg-*. When the plural endings in *-en* are added to the stem, the double consonant is restored in order to show the closed syllable of the stem: *ik zit* (I sit) but *wij zitten* (we sit), *ik leg* (I lay) but *wij leggen* (we lay).

3. When the final consonant of the infinitive is either *v* or *z*, it is changed to *f* and *s* respectively to give the stem form: *beven* (to tremble) has the stem *beef-*, *reizen* (to travel) has the stem *reis-*. Before the plural *-en* endings, *f* and *s* become *v* and *z*: *ik beef* (I tremble) but *wij beven* (we tremble), *ik reis* (I travel) but *wij reizen* (we travel):

ik	maak	kus	reis	I make, kiss, travel
jij	maakt	kust	reist	you make, kiss, travel
hij	maakt	kust	reist	he makes, kisses, travels
u	maakt	kust	reist	you make, kiss, travel
wij	maken	kussen	reizen	we make, kiss, travel
jullie	maken	kussen	reizen	you make, kiss, travel
zij	maken	kussen	reizen	they make, kiss, travel

The student should note carefully the following points when using the present tense:

1. The polite *u*-form always takes the ending *-t*, whether one is referring to one or more persons: *u komt* (you come), singular or plural depending upon the context.

2. When the pronoun *jij* (*je*) follows its verb, the *-t* ending on the verb is dropped: *jij zingt* (you sing), but *zing je?* (are you singing?).

3. A few verbs with stems ending in *-d*, notably *snijden* (to cut), *houden* (to hold), and *rijden* (to ride), often drop the *-d* in the first person singular: *ik snij* (I cut), *ik hou* (I hold), *ik rij* (I ride). In the second person singular these verbs regularly drop the *-dt* when the pronoun subject follows: *snij je?* (are you cutting?), *hou je?* (are you holding?), *rij je?* (are you riding?).

4. In keeping with the general rules for spelling, verbs whose stem ends in *-t* do not add the *-t* ending in the second and third persons singular: *laten* (to let), *ik laat* (I let), *jij laat* (you let), *hij laat* (he lets).

5. The verb *komen* changes the length of its vowel from short in the singular to long in the plural. The irregularity in pronunciation is reflected in the spelling: *ik kom, wij komen.*

Hebben and Zijn

The verbs *hebben* (to have) and *zijn* (to be) are irregular in the present tense:

ik	heb	ben	I have, am
jij	hebt	bent	you have, are
hij	heeft	is	he has, is
u	hebt	bent	you have, are
wij	hebben	zijn	we have, are
jullie	hebben	zijn	you have, are
zij	hebben	zijn	they have, are

When *jij* (*je*) follows these verbs, the -*t* ending is dropped: *heb je?* (do you have?), *ben je?* (are you?). The forms *u heeft* and *u is* also occur in place of *u hebt* (you have) and *u bent* (you are), but they are much less common. *Zullen*, another verb that is irregular in the present, will be considered later.

The Progressive

There are no present tense forms in Dutch to compare to the English progressive (I am singing, he is playing, they are running) or emphatic (I do sing, he does play, they do run) forms. Thus Dutch *ik zing* may, depending upon context, mean either "I sing," "I am singing," or "I do sing." Progressive forms in English focus upon an activity as it is taking place. To indicate action in progress Dutch often uses (appropriately to the situation) the verbs *liggen* (to lie), *lopen* (to run OR walk), *staan* (to stand), or *zitten* (to sit) followed by *te* and the infinitive:

Hij ligt te slapen.

He is sleeping (that is, he is lying down and sleeping while in that position).

Zij staan te praten.

They are talking (that is, they are standing and talking as they stand).

Wij zitten te lezen.
We are reading (that is, we are sitting and as we sit we are also reading).

Dutch has no specific verb forms or combination of verb forms to render the English emphatic. Generally adverbs are used to modify the sense of the verb or to lend emphasis to it.

The Imperative

The imperative form of a verb expresses an order or command: "Come home quickly," "Do your homework." In English the imperative form of the verb is identical with the infinitive. In Dutch the stem form of the verb generally functions as the imperative for both the singular and plural. No ending is added:

luisteren (to listen)	Luister goed!	Listen carefully!
wachten (to wait)	Wacht op ons!	Wait for us!
nemen (to take)	Neem dit boek!	Take this book!

In polite address, both singular and plural, the -*t* ending is added to the stem form and the pronoun *u* follows. The addition of the pronoun tends to soften the command and make it less abrupt:

lezen (to read)	Leest u wat langzamer!
	Read more slowly!
blijven (to remain)	Blijft u met ons!
	Stay with us!

The imperative of the verb *zijn* (to be) is irregular: *wees* (*weest u*)!

The Simple Past Tense

1. English and Dutch are related languages with a shared history, and this is nowhere more apparent than in the formation of the various tenses of the verb. As in English, Dutch verbs fall into two main classes, usually called *weak* and *strong*. Strong verbs in both languages undergo an internal vowel change in the past tense. Note the English "I drive—I drove," "I sing—I sang." Weak verbs in English and Dutch signal the past tense by the addition of a suffix. Note the English "I play—I played," "I call—I called." To form the past tense of a weak verb in Dutch, simply add to the stem the ending -*te* (-*de*) for all persons of the singular, and -*ten* (-*den*) for all persons of the plural. When the stem of a verb ends in *p, t, k, f, s,* or *ch,* add the endings -*te* / -*ten*; in all other cases use -*de* / -*den*:

hakken (to chop) STEM: hak-
| ik (jij, hij, u) | hak*te* | I (you, he, you) | chopped |
| wij (jullie, zij) | hak*ten* | we (you, they) | chopped |

praten (to talk) STEM: praat-
| ik (jij, hij, u) | praat*te* | I (you, he, you) | talked |
| wij (jullie, zij) | praat*ten* | we (you, they) | talked |

trouwen (to marry) STEM: trouw-
| ik (jij, hij, u) | trouw*de* | I (you, he, you) | married |
| wij (jullie, zij) | trouw*den* | we (you, they) | married |

delen (to divide) STEM: deel-
| ik (jij, hij, u) | deel*de* | I (you, he, you) | divided |
| wij (jullie, zij) | deel*den* | we (you, they) | divided |

Note that verbs that have either *v* or *z* as their final consonants (before the -*en* ending of the infinitive) change these to *f* and *s* in the stem form and then take the endings -*de* and -*den*:

geloven (to believe) STEM: geloof-
| ik (jij, hij, u) | geloof*de* | I (you, he, you) | believed |
| wij (jullie, zij) | geloof*den* | we (you, they) | believed |

reizen (to travel) STEM: reis-
| ik (jij, hij, u) | reis*de* | I (you, he, you) | traveled |
| wij (jullie, zij) | reis*den* | we (you, they) | traveled |

2. In contrast to weak verbs, strong verbs employ an internal vowel change to show the past tense. The new stem resulting from the vowel change functions as the past tense form for all persons of the singular. Plural forms take the ending -*en*:

bijten (to bite)
| ik (jij, hij, u) | beet | I (you, he, you) | bit |
| wij (jullie, zij) | beten | we (you, they) | bit |

drinken (to drink)
| ik (jij, hij, u) | dronk | I (you, he, you) | drank |
| wij (jullie, zij) | dronken | we (you, they) | drank |

gieten (to pour)

| ik (jij, hij, u) | goot | I (you, he, you) | poured |
| wij (jullie, zij) | goten | we (you, they) | poured |

Historically, strong verbs belong to one of seven classes, each class having its own pattern of internal vowel change. In modern Dutch the classes are still recognizable, although the force of analogy and leveling has caused many alterations. The beginning student is encouraged to learn the vowel change for each verb individually rather than to attempt learning the modern strong verb classes (with their several subclasses). A list of the most important strong verbs with their past tenses can be found in Appendix C. The list is followed by a sampling of strong verbs categorized according to class.

A few strong verbs show a slight irregularity in the past tense in that the quantity of the stem vowel changes from short in the singular to long in the plural:

eten (to eat)

| ik (jij, hij, u) | at (short *a*) | I (you, he, you) | ate |
| wij (jullie, zij) | aten (long *a*) | we (you, they) | ate |

breken (to break)

| ik (jij, hij, u) | brak (short *a*) | I (you, he, you) | broke |
| ij (jullie, zij) | braken (long *a*) | we (you, they) | broke |

3. In addition to weak and strong verbs Dutch has a number of irregular verbs. For the purposes of the present grammar an irregular verb is any verb that does not fit into the conjugation patterns of weak and strong verbs. The past tense must be learned separately for each irregular verb. Irregular verbs take no ending in the singular of the past; in the plural they add *-en* for all persons. Note the following irregular verbs and consult Appendix D for a list of the most common irregular verbs in Dutch:

gaan (to go)

| ik (jij, hij, u) | ging | I (you, he, you) | went |
| wij (jullie, zij) | gingen | we (you, they) | went |

weten (to know)

| ik (jij, hij, u) | wist | I (you, he, you) | knew |
| wij (jullie, zij) | wisten | we (you, they) | knew |

denken (to think)

| ik (jij, hij, u) | dacht | I (you, he, you) | thought |
| wij (jullie, zij) | dachten | we (you, they) | thought |

The verbs *hebben* and *zijn* are both irregular in the past tense:

| ik (jij, hij, u) | had | was | I (you, he, you) had, was/were |
| wij (jullie, zij) | hadden | waren | we (you, they) had, were |

It should be stressed that the student cannot tell whether a given verb is weak, strong, or irregular simply by looking at the infinitive form. Grammars and dictionaries will indicate whether a verb is strong or irregular. In the case of weak verbs the student needs no further information.

The Present Perfect Tense

The present perfect tense is a compound tense in Dutch, as it is in English. Note the English "I have thought," "He has gone," "We have seen." In Dutch the present perfect tense consists of one working verb—the present tense of *hebben* or *zijn*—and one inactive verb form: the past participle.* We will discuss the past participle first.

The Past Participle

Weak, strong, and irregular verbs form their past participles in different ways:

1. Weak verbs add to the stem the prefix *ge-* and a suffix, either *-t* or *-d*. The suffix *-t* is applied when the stem ends in *p*, *t*, *k*, *f* (except for *f* derived from *v* of the infinitive), *s* (except for *s* derived from *z* of the infinitive), or *ch* (see the rules for the for-

---

* The basic forms of a verb from which all the tenses can be derived are called the "principal parts." The principal parts of a Dutch verb are the **infinitive**, the **simple past**, and the **past participle**. In the case of weak verbs one need only know the infinitive to be able to derive all other forms; for strong and irregular verbs, however, it is necessary to know all three principal parts. And so, for example, the principal parts of the verb *krijgen* (to get, receive) are: *krijgen* (infinitive), *kreeg* (past), *gekregen* (past participle). The principal parts of the most common strong verbs can be found in Appendix A; the principal parts of the most common irregular verbs are listed in Appendix D.

The principal parts alone are not sufficient for learning the irregular present tense of a few verbs (*zijn*, *hebben*, etc.). These irregular presents are supplied at the appropriate places in the present grammar.

mation of the past tense for weak verbs); in all other cases the suffix is -d:

dopen (to christen)	STEM: doop-	PAST PART.: gedoopt
scherpen (to sharpen)	STEM: scherp-	PAST PART.: gescherpt
eisen (to demand)	STEM: eis-	PAST PART.: geëist
horen (to hear)	STEM: hoor-	PAST PART.: gehoord
stellen (to place)	STEM: stel-	PAST PART.: gesteld
leven (to live)	STEM: leef-	PAST PART.: geleefd
leiden (to lead)	STEM: leid-	PAST PART.: geleid
niezen (to sneeze)	STEM: nies-	PAST PART.: geniesd

2. Strong verbs also add the prefix *ge-*. These verbs, however, often undergo a change in their stem vowels, and they all take the suffix *-en*:

krijgen (to get, receive)	PAST PART.: gekregen
bieden (to offer)	PAST PART.: geboden
sluiten (to close)	PAST PART.: gesloten
zingen (to sing)	PAST PART.: gezongen
stelen (to steal)	PAST PART.: gestolen
lezen (to read)	PAST PART.: gelezen
lopen (to walk)	PAST PART.: gelopen
dragen (to carry)	PAST PART.: gedragen

3. Irregular verbs also add the prefix *ge-* in the past participle. In addition, they may have a vowel or consonant change in the stem. Some take *-t* (*-d*) as their suffix, others take *-en*:

brengen (to bring)	PAST PART.: gebracht
doen (to do)	PAST PART.: gedaan
vriezen (to freeze)	PAST PART.: gevroren

4. The past participles of *hebben* and *zijn* are *gehad* and *geweest*, respectively.

5. There is an important exception to the rule for placing the prefix *ge-* on the past participle of weak, strong, and irregular verbs. No verb, regardless of its class, adds the *ge-* prefix if it already includes an *inseparable* (*unstressed*) *prefix*. The inseparable prefixes are: *be-*, *er-*, *ge-*, *her-*, *ont-*, and *ver-*:

bedoelen [WEAK] (to mean, intend)	PAST PART.: bedoeld
ontmoeten [WEAK] (to meet)	PAST PART.: ontmoet

ervaren [STRONG] (to learn, find out)   PAST PART.: ervaren
vermijden [STRONG] (to avoid)   PAST PART.: vermeden
bedenken [IRREGULAR] (to consider)   PAST PART.: bedacht
herkennen [IRREGULAR] (to recognize)   PAST PART.: herkend

6. If, on the other hand, the verb has a *separable* (*stressed*) *prefix*, such as *aan-*, *door-*, or *op-* (among many others), the participial *-ge-* is inserted between the prefix and the stem of the verb:

aannemen [STRONG] (to accept)
PAST PART.: aangenomen

doorbrengen [IRREGULAR] (to pass, spend)
PAST PART.: doorgebracht

opbellen [WEAK] (to call up)
PAST PART.: opgebeld*

Verb prefixes, both separable and inseparable, will be discussed later in this chapter.

Forming the Present Perfect

As noted above, the present perfect tense employs one working verb form, that being the present tense of *hebben* or *zijn*. Most verbs require the working verb *hebben*, which is used with:

1. All transitive verbs (a transitive verb is one that takes a direct object):

Ik heb hem gezien.	I have seen him.
Hij heeft zijn vriend geholpen.	He has helped his friend.
Heb je een auto gekocht?	Have you bought a car?

2. Intransitive verbs (that is, verbs that do not take a direct object), when they do *not* express a change of location or state:

Hij heeft lang geslapen.	He has slept a long time.
Ik heb in Den Haag gewoond.	I have lived in The Hague.
Zij hebben hartelijk gelachen.	They have laughed heartily.

A number of verbs take *zijn* for the present perfect in certain circumstances, while a few always require *zijn*.

---

* Since the final syllable of *opgebeld* is closed without it (see **Spelling**, p. 8), the second *l* is redundant and drops out.

1. When an intransitive verb describes a change of location or condition it requires the working verb *zijn*:

De trein is vertrokken.	The train has departed.
Hij is ingeslapen.	He has fallen asleep (change of state).
Wij zijn naar Utrecht gefietst.	We bicycled to Utrecht.
Zij zijn gestorven.	They have died.

2. With the exception of a few verbs such as *gaan* (to go) and *komen* (to come), which always require the working verb *zijn*, verbs of motion take *zijn* when the motion described is directed toward a destination; *hebben* is used when these verbs express motion as an undirected activity:

Hij heeft een tijd gewandeld.
He walked for a while (activity).

BUT: Hij is naar de stad gewandeld.
He walked to the city (destination).

Ik heb nooit gevlogen.
I have never flown (activity).

BUT: Ik ben naar Amsterdam gevlogen.
I flew to Amsterdam (destination).

3. Exceptions to the rules for *hebben* and *zijn* are the two verbs *blijven* (to remain) and *zijn* (to be). Both of these verbs, contrary to what one would expect, require the working verb *zijn*:

Ik ben thuis gebleven.	I remained at home.
Hij is er nooit geweest.	He has never been there.

4. The verb *vergeten* (to forget) provides an interesting case of the distribution of *hebben* and *zijn*. When *vergeten* means "to forget" in the sense that someone no longer knows something, the working verb is *zijn*; when, however, *vergeten* merely indicates negligence, the working verb is *hebben*:

Ik ben zijn naam vergeten.	I have forgotten his name (I no longer know).
Ik heb mijn boek vergeten.	I have forgotten my book (negligence).

Present Perfect: Word Order and Usage

Since *hebben* and *zijn* function as the working verb in present perfect constructions, they occupy verb position in the sentence. The inactive verb form, the past participle, is generally placed last in the sentence or clause. The student is encouraged at this point to review Dutch sentence types as outlined on pp. 10–12.

Type I, Sequence 1 :	Wij hebben hem vaak gezien.
	We have often seen him.
Type I, Sequence 2 :	Gisteren ben ik in Delft geweest.
	Yesterday I was in Delft.
Type II :	Heeft hij de auto al verkocht?
	Has he sold the car already?
Type III :	Ik weet niet of hij al aangekomen is.
	I do not know if he has arrived yet.

In contrast to English, Dutch does not draw a sharp distinction in meaning between the simple past tense and the present perfect tense. English "I saw" and "I have seen" are not interchangeable, and no native speaker would say "I have seen him last night." In Dutch, the distinction between these two tenses tends to be one of style rather than of meaning. As a general rule the Dutch present perfect is the most common way to express past time, and thus can be translated as a simple past or present perfect in English as the context requires. The Dutch simple past is usually employed for narrating a series of events that occurred in the past.

To indicate action begun in the past and continuing into the present, English uses a progressive form of the present perfect tense. Note sentences of the type "I have been living here for years," "He has been teaching in New York since 1970." For sentences of this type Dutch uses the *present tense*, almost always accompanied either by the adverb *al* (already) or a prepositional phrase introduced by *sinds* (since):

Ik woon al twee jaar in Edam.
I have been living in Edam for two years.

Sinds wanneer wonen zij in Nederland?
How long (Since when) have they been living in the Netherlands?

The Past Perfect Tense

The Dutch past perfect tense consists of the simple past tense of *hebben* (sing. *had,* pl. *hadden*) or *zijn* (sing. *was,* pl. *waren*) and the past participle of the verb. *Zijn* is used by the same verbs that use it in the present perfect tense. The past perfect tense is used the same way in Dutch as it is in English, that is, to refer to a past action that occurred before some other past action:

Zij had de boeken niet gevonden.
She had not found the books.

Wij hadden in Leiden gestudeerd.
We had studied in Leiden.

Nadat wij haar broer bezocht hadden, gingen wij naar de stad.
After we had visited her brother, we went downtown.

The Future Tense

Both English and Dutch form the future tense in the same way. English uses the working verbs "shall" or "will" and the infinitive, while Dutch employs the present tense forms of the working verb *zullen* with the infinitive. These forms of *zullen* are:

ik	zal	wij	zullen
jij	zult (zal)	jullie	zullen
hij	zal	zij	zullen
u	zult		

Note that *jij zal* occurs less commonly than *jij zult*; in inversions the *-t* on *zult* is dropped: *jij zult* but *zul je?*

When *zullen* combines with an infinitive to form the future tense, it occupies the position of the working verb and the infinitive comes at the end of the sentence or clause:

Wij zullen met de auto gaan.   We will go by car.
Zal hij hier op ons wachten?   Will he wait for us here?
De reis zal twee uur duren.   The trip will last two hours.
Wat zal me nu overkomen?   What will happen to me now?

2. In English the future tense is sometimes used to indicate present probability. For example, one might respond to a ring of the telephone with "That will be John," or to a knock on the door with "That will be my father." The Dutch future tense can also signal present probability. When it does, the adverb *wel* is usually added to the sentence:

Zij zullen het wel weten.   They probably know it.

3. It is quite common in Dutch to use present tense forms to express future action, particularly when it is clear from the context that the future is being referred to (note the English "We are leaving for the beach tomorrow"):

Hoe lang blijft hij in Nederland?
How long will he stay in the Netherlands?

Morgen gaan wij naar Rotterdam.
We are going (will go) to Rotterdam tomorrow.

De trein vertrekt om elf uur.
The train is leaving (will leave) at 11:00.

Very frequently sentences of this type contain an adverb or prepositional phrase referring to future time.

4. Sentences of the type "We are going dancing," and "He is going to help us" focus on the beginning of an action in future time. Dutch has an analogous construction in which it uses *gaan* as a working verb with an accompanying infinitive:

Hij gaat een brief schrijven.   He is going to write a letter.
Wij gaan morgen zwemmen.   We are going swimming
                                 tomorrow.

The Future Perfect Tense

The future perfect tense, uncommon in both languages, indicates action completed at some point in the future. Note the English "We will have seen him," "They will have gone home by then." In Dutch the working verb *zullen* combines with two inactive verb forms: the past participle of the relevant verb, plus the infinitive of *hebben* or *zijn* (*zijn* for the verbs that use it in the present perfect and past perfect):

Hij zal de krant gelezen hebben.
He will have read the newspaper.

Zij zullen naar Breda gegaan zijn.
They will have gone to Breda.

The Conditional Mood

The conditional mood expresses doubt, uncertainty, or unreality (in English, characterized by the use of "would"). In Dutch, as in English, the conditional has largely replaced the subjunctive, of which only a few traces remain. In a conditional construction the working verb is a past tense form of *zullen*:

ik (jij, hij)   zou   wij (jullie, zij)   zouden
u   zou(dt)

The conditional occurs in only two tenses or time frames: the present, which often has future reference, and the past.

The **present conditional** consists of the working verb *zou/zouden* and the relevant infinitive:

Hij zou graag thuis blijven.
He would like to (OR: would gladly) stay home.

Wij zouden dat huis niet kopen.
We would not buy that house.

Als ik jij was, zou ik hem later opbellen.
If I were you, I would call him later.

The **past conditional** consists of the working verb *zou/zouden*, the past participle, and *hebben* or *zijn*:

Ik zou dat huis niet gekocht hebben.
I would not have bought that house.

Hij zou graag thuis gebleven zijn.
He would have liked to stay at home.

Als hij harder gewerkt had, zou ik hem geholpen hebben.
If he had worked harder, I would have helped him.

The Passive Voice

In the **active voice** the subject of a sentence performs the action: "He sees her," "The man bought a new house." In the **passive voice** the subject of the sentence is the recipient of the action: "He is seen by her," "A new house was bought by the man." In a passive construction the actual doer of the action is often expressed in a prepositional phrase introduced in English by "by."

In English, the passive voice is formed by using the working verb " to be " and the past participle: " He is seen; he was seen; he will be seen; he has been seen," etc. Dutch uses one of three working verbs: *worden* (to become) for the present and past tense; *zullen* for the future and future perfect; and *zijn* for the present perfect and past perfect. These working verbs combine with inactive forms to convey the various passive tenses.

1. The **present passive** consists of the present tense of *worden* and the past participle of the relevant verb:

Zij wordt door haar vader gezien.
She is seen by her father.

Zij worden door ons geholpen.
They are being helped by us.

Note that the agent is expressed by *door* (through, by) in Dutch.

2. The **past passive** consists of the past tense of *worden* and the past participle of the relevant verb. The past tense forms of *worden* are singular *werd* and plural *werden*.

Het geld werd betaald.	The money was paid.
Zij werden door hem geholpen.	They were being helped by him.

3. The **future passive** combines the present tense of *zullen* with the past participle of the relevant verb and the inactive form *worden*:

Het huis zal gebouwd worden.
The house will be built.

De liederen zullen gezongen worden.
The songs will be sung.

4. The **future perfect passive** combines the present tense of *zullen* with the past participle of the relevant verb and the inactive form *zijn*:

Het huis zal gebouwd zijn.
The house will have been built.

De liederen zullen gezongen zijn.
The songs will have been sung.

5. The **present perfect passive** consists of the present tense of *zijn* and the past participle of the relevant verb:

> Het brood is gebakken.
> The bread has been baked. (OR: The bread is baked.)
> De brieven zijn geschreven.
> The letters have been written. (OR: The letters are written.)

As the alternative translations of the last two sample sentences indicate, the construction *zijn* with the past participle of a transitive verb has two possible meanings: (1) it may indicate a real passive construction in which an activity is described, as in "The bread has been baked," or (2) it may indicate an apparent passive in which a state is described, as in "The bread is baked." In the latter case the adverb *al* (already) would fill out the meaning of the sentence. The distinction in meaning between real and apparent passive can be further seen in the two English sentences "The door was closed," which could mean either that someone was closing it (activity) or else that it was shut, i.e., someone had already closed it (state), and "The door was being closed," indicating only activity, not state.

6. The **past perfect passive** consists of the past tense of *zijn* (sing. *was*, pl. *waren*) and the past participle of the relevant verb:

> Het boek was vertaald.
> The book had been translated.
> De namen waren opgeschreven.
> The names had been written down.

7. The **conditional passive** is formed with the past tense of *zullen* (*zou/zouden*) as the working verb, plus the past participle and *worden*:

> Als het oven heet was, zou het koek gebakken worden.
> If the oven were hot, the cake would be baked.

8. The **conditional perfect passive** combines *zou/zouden*, the past participle and *zijn*:

> Als ik hier geweest was, zou het raam niet gebroken zijn.
> If I had been here, the window would not have been broken.

Dutch speakers and writers often find the passive voice awkward and cumbersome. One common way of avoiding the passive is the use of an active construction with *men* (one) as the subject. As noted on p. 41, *men* is an indefinite pronoun that can be translated variously as "one," "you," "they" or "people." The following examples show passive constructions with their active equivalents (note that *men* always takes a singular verb):

Hij wordt geholpen. / Men helpt hem.
He is being helped.

De sleutels zijn pas gisteren gevonden. / Men heeft de sleutels pas gisteren gevonden.
The keys were found only yesterday.

Although the passive voice construction is generally, and logically, restricted to transitive verbs, certain *impersonal passive* constructions can be formed with either transitive or intransitive verbs. These constructions have no grammatical subject, are often introduced by *er* (there), and focus on general activity rather than the person(s) performing the action:

Er wordt gezongen en gedanst.
There is singing and dancing (going on).

Er wordt in ons huis hard gewerkt.
We work hard in our house.

Er wordt in onze scholen te veel gerookt.
There is too much smoking in our schools.

Note that sentences of this type resist a literal translation: "There is sung and danced," etc.

Kunnen, Moeten, Mogen, and Willen

The verbs *kunnen, moeten, mogen,* and *willen* deserve particular attention. They often function as working verbs and yet do not themselves describe action. They indicate rather the aspect, manner, or mode of an action that is signaled by an accompanying inactive verb form. In the English sentences "I want to go home" and "I must see him" the working verbs are "want" and "must"; the actual action, however, is expressed through the inactive verb forms "go" and "see." In both English and Dutch there are several so-called "modal" verbs, verbs that do not describe activity and yet function as working verbs. In Dutch these verbs are *kunnen, moeten, mogen,* and *willen,* and their forms are irregular.

kunnen (to be able, can)

PRESENT: ik kan, jij kunt (kan), hij kan, u kunt
        wij (jullie, zij) kunnen
PAST: ik (jij, hij, u) kon
        wij (jullie, zij) konden

Ik kan (kon) mijn hoed niet vinden.
I can't (couldn't) find my hat.

Wij kunnen (konden) niet langer hier blijven.
We can't (couldn't) stay here any longer.

moeten (to have to, be obliged to, must)

PRESENT: ik (jij, hij, u) moet
        wij (jullie, zij) moeten
PAST: ik (jij, hij, u) moest
        wij (jullie, zij) moesten

Ik moet (moest) vaak Nederlands spreken.
Often I must (had to) speak Dutch.

Zij moeten (moesten) alleen komen.
They have to (had to) come alone.

mogen (to be allowed to, may)

PRESENT: ik (jij, hij, u) mag
        wij (jullie, zij) mogen
PAST: ik (jij, hij, u) mocht
        wij (jullie, zij) mochten

Ik mag (mocht) koffie niet drinken.
I am (was) not allowed to drink coffee.

Wij mogen (mochten) bij hem logeren.
We may (were allowed to) stay at his house.

Note that *mogen* sometimes indicates possibility rather than permission:

Dat mag waar zijn.   That may be true.

willen (to want)

PRESENT: ik wil, jij wilt (wil), hij wil, u wilt
wij (jullie, zij) willen
PAST: ik (jij, hij, u) wilde (OR: wou)
wij (jullie, zij) wilden

Hij wil (wilde) Engels leren.
He wants (wanted) to learn English.

Zij willen (wilden) melk kopen.
They want (wanted) to buy milk.

Frequently infinitives accompanying *kunnen, moeten, mogen,* or *willen* are omitted when the meaning is already clear from the context. This is particularly the case with verbs of going or "to do":

Waar wil je nou heen?	Where do you want *to go* now?
Ik moet al morgen weg.	I must *leave* tomorrow.
Hij mag niet naar school.	He is not permitted *to go* to school.
Ik kan het niet.	I can't *do* it.
Kan dat?	Is that possible?
	(LITERALLY: Can it *be done?*)

In the sentences above, the English words in italic are not expressed in the Dutch. In the future tense *kunnen, moeten, mogen,* and *willen* appear in the inactive (infinitive) form, giving way to the working verb *zullen.* The result is a so-called **double infinitive** construction:

Wij zullen de tentoonstelling willen bezoeken.
We will want to visit the exhibit.

Hij zal ons niet kunnen helpen.
He will not be able to help us.

In the present perfect and past perfect tenses the working verb is *hebben* and again a double infinitive construction results:*

---

* In the perfect tenses, this double infinitive construction is also used with *laten* (see p. 64), and, in addition, with *lopen, staan, zitten,* etc. (see p. 47) to express a progressive meaning:

Ik heb mijn horloge laten repareren.   I have had my watch repaired.
Zij heeft de hele dag zitten schrijven.   She has been writing all day.

Ik heb (had) het mogen doen.
I was (had been) allowed to do it.

Hij heeft (had) om hulp moeten vragen.
He had (had had) to ask for help.

Wij hebben (hadden) haar niet kunnen verstaan.
We were not (had not been) able to understand her.

If *kunnen, moeten, mogen,* or *willen* occur in the present or past perfect tense without another infinitive, they then take on the inactive form of the past participle. The past participles of these verbs are *gekund, gemoeten, gemoogd,* and *gewild,* respectively:

Wij hebben (hadden) het altijd gekund.
We have (had) always been able (to do it).

Ik heb (had) het niet gewild.
I did not want (had not wanted) it.

It is common in constructions of this type that a verb of doing is understood. Note, for example, the first of the two sample sentences.

Laten

The verb *laten* (past *liet/lieten,* past participle *gelaten*) has a number of important meanings and uses, two of which will be discussed here.

1. A basic meaning of *laten* is "to let, allow." In this sense it frequently indicates a suggestion on the part of the speaker:

Laten wij even kijken.	Let's just take a look.
Laten wij nu dit lied zingen.	Let us sing this song now.

Note that the subject form of the pronoun is used in Dutch (*wij* "we") and not the object form as in English ("Let *us* . . . ").

2. *Laten* may also mean "to cause, have done" and in this meaning functions grammatically much like the modal verbs just discussed:

Ik laat mijn auto repareren.
I have my car repaired.

Ik liet mijn auto repareren.
I had my car repaired.

Ik heb mijn auto laten repareren.
I have had my car repaired.
Ik had mijn auto laten repareren.
I had had my car repaired.
Ik zal mijn auto laten repareren.
I will have my car repaired.

Be careful not to confuse the following:

Ik laat mijn auto repareren.
I have my car repaired [by someone else].
Ik heb mijn auto gerepareerd.
I have repaired my car [by myself].
Ik liet mijn auto repareren.
I had my car repaired.
Ik had mijn auto gerepareerd.
I had repaired my car.

Prefixed Verbs

Inseparable (unstressed) prefixes were mentioned earlier in the chapter with regard to forming past participles. An inseparable prefix remains attached to a verb in all its active and inactive forms. There is, however, another class of prefixes, the **separable (stressed)** prefixes, that may occupy several positions in a sentence. Some of the more common separable prefixes are: *aan-*, *af-*, *in-*, *mee-*, *na-*, *op-*, and *uit-*.

Prefixes, separable and inseparable, alter the meaning of the verbs to which they are attached. It is often possible to discern the meaning of a separable-prefix verb from its component parts: *brengen* (to bring), *meebrengen* (to bring along); *staan* (to stand), *opstaan* (to stand up). Some separable-prefix verbs are not so easily understood from their components, however: *stellen* (to put, place), *uitstellen* (to postpone); *geven* (to give), *uitgeven* (to publish). The meaning of an inseparable-prefix verb is generally not obvious from its parts: *denken* (to think), *verdenken* (to suspect); *keren* (to turn), *bekeren* (to convert).

Note that verbs with prefixes are always listed in dictionaries under their prefix. A separable prefix remains attached to its verb when the verb appears in an inactive form (infinitive or

past participle), or when an active form of the verb occurs at
the end of a sentence or clause (Type III word order). Normally, a working form of a verb occupies second position in the
sentence and its separable prefix is placed at or near the end of
the sentence. Note the following sentences using the verb *opbellen*
(to call up):

> Ik bel hem nu op.
> I'll call him up now.
>
> Bel je hem morgen op?
> Will you call him tomorrow?
>
> Ik heb hem al gisteren opgebeld.
> I already called him up yesterday.
>
> Ik zal hem morgen opbellen.
> I will call him up tomorrow.

In the next two examples note that the prefix *op-* is separated
from the infinitive form *bellen*. This exception to the general rule
occurs: (1) when, in Type III word order, the working form of
a modal verb comes between the prefix and its verb at the end
of a sentence or clause; and (2) when, in constructions of
purpose with *om* . . . *te* " (in order) to," prefix and infinitive are
separated by *te*:

> Ik weet dat ik hem morgen op moet bellen.
> I know that I must call him tomorrow.
>
> Ik ben van plan om hem morgen op te bellen.
> I intend to call him tomorrow.

Reflexive Verbs

The forms and use of reflexive pronouns came under dis-
cussion on pp. 39–40. It should be stressed that Dutch makes
more use of reflexive constructions than does English. In the following sentences note how Dutch requires a reflexive pronoun
object while English does not:

wassen (to wash)	Hij wast zich.
	He gets washed (He washes himself).
scheren (to shave)	Ik scheer me.
	I shave.

aankleden (to dress) Zij kleden zich aan.
They get dressed (They dress).

In English it is understood that the subject is acting upon itself; in Dutch this must be expressed through the reflexive pronoun. In the Dutch sentences above, omission of the reflexive pronoun would leave the sentence grammatically incomplete and potentially ambiguous.

There are several verbs in Dutch that are used primarily (though not exclusively) in reflexive constructions the English equivalents of which are not reflexive:*

zich verheugen (to be glad, Ik verheug me op zaterdag.
look forward) I look forward to Saturday.

zich verbazen (to be surprised) Hij verbaast zich erover.
He is surprised about it.

zich haasten (to hurry) Wij moeten ons haasten.
We must hurry.

Finally, there is the category of a purely reflexive verb, one that can only be used reflexively. Perhaps the only commonly occurring, exclusively reflexive verb is *zich vergissen* " to make a mistake ":

Ik vergis me. I am mistaken.
Jij vergist je. You are mistaken.
Wij vergissen ons. We are mistaken.

Impersonal Verbs

Impersonal verbs denote action by an unspecified agent and are used in the third person singular. We have already noted the use of impersonal verbs in the passive voice (e.g., *er wordt gezongen* " there is singing "). In addition, like English, Dutch makes use of impersonal verbs for describing natural phenomena:

Het regent. It is raining.
Het sneeuwt. It is snowing.

---

* *Verheugen*, *verbazen*, and *haasten*, when not reflexive, are transitive verbs meaning, respectively, " to make glad," " to surprise," and " to make [someone] hurry."

Het hagelt.	It is hailing.
Het waait.	It (the wind) is blowing.

In a few cases a Dutch impersonal construction has no impersonal equivalent in English:

Het spijt me dat . . . .
I am sorry [LITERALLY: It causes me regret] that . . . .

What is the subject in English is here expressed as the object in Dutch, the Dutch subject being the impersonal *het* (it).

CONJUNCTIONS

A few conjunctions in Dutch introduce clauses that require Type I (or Type II) word order. Grammars generally refer to these conjunctions as **coordinating** and the clauses they introduce as **independent**. Most Dutch conjunctions, however, introduce clauses requiring Type III word order, that is, word order that relegates the working verb to last position in the clause. Generally these conjunctions are called **subordinating**, and the clauses they introduce are designated **dependent**. The student is perhaps best advised simply to note the few conjunctions that require Type I (or Type II) word order and to assume that all others will require Type III word order. Use Type I or II word order after the following conjunctions:

en (and) of (or—but not when it means "whether")
maar (but) want (because, since, for)

Note the position (Type I) of the underlined verbs in the following sentences:

Hij gaat mee, maar ik <u>blijf</u> thuis.
He is going along, but I'm staying home.

Ik blijf thuis, want het <u>regent</u> hard.
I'm staying home, since it's raining hard.

Use Type III word order after the following, and almost all other, conjunctions:

al (although, even though)
als (when, if)
alsof (as though, as if)
daar (because)
dat (that)
hoe (how)
hoewel (although)
indien (if, in case)

nadat (after)
nu (now that)
of (whether, if)
ofschoon (although)
omdat (because)
opdat (in order that)
sedert (since [temporal])
sinds (since [temporal]

terwijl (while, whereas)   wanneer (when, if)
toen (when)   zoals (as, like)
tot(dat) (until)   zodat (so that)
voor(dat) (before)

Note the position (Type III) of the underlined verbs in the following sentences:

Hij komt niet, omdat hij geen tijd <u>heeft</u>.
He's not coming, since he has no time.

Ik wist niet dat Piet al vertrokken <u>was</u>.
I didn't know that Piet had left already.

Ik vroeg hem of hij de film al gezien <u>had</u>.
I asked him if he had seen the film yet.

PREPOSITIONS

Prepositions in Dutch function much as they do in English. The nouns they govern do not change their form in any way, while pronouns are put into the objective case:

de auto (the car)
met de auto (by car)
het huis (the house)
achter het huis (behind the house)
ik (I)
met mij (OR: me) (with me)
hij (he)
achter hem (behind him)

The most common Dutch prepositions are as follows:

aan (on, upon, at, to)
achter (behind)
beneden (beneath, below)
bij (by, with, near)
binnen (within)
boven (above, over)
buiten (outside, out of)
door (through)
gedurende (during)
in (in, into, at, on)
langs (along)
met (with)
na (after)
naar (to, according to)
naast (next to)
om (around, at [time], for)
omstreeks (about, approximately)
ondanks (in spite of)
onder (underneath, among)

op (on, upon, in, at)
over (over, on top of, across)
sedert (since [temporal])
sinds (since [temporal])
te (at, in)
tegen (against)
tot (to, up to, until)
tussen (between)
uit (out of, from)
van (from, of, by)
vanaf (from)
voor (for, in front of, before)
zonder (without)

As is the case in most languages, so also in Dutch the choice of prepositions in given situations tends to be highly idiomatic. This is particularly noticeable when prepositions express relationships beyond the purely temporal or spatial. A few examples of differences between Dutch and English will suffice in demonstrating this:

zeggen tegen (to say to)
wachten op (to wait for)
verliefd op (in love with)
zoeken naar (to look for)
lachen om (to laugh about)
denken aan (to think about [OR: of])
met de trein (by train)
met vacantie (on vacation)
feliciteren met (to congratulate on)
voorbereiden op (to prepare for)

No reliable rules can be formulated for the proper choice of prepositions. The student must simply note instances of divergent usage as they occur.

Prepositional compounds, which were discussed on pp. 38–39, will be reviewed here, since this is one point of Dutch grammar that seems to cause difficulties for English speakers. Dutch prepositions may not govern personal pronoun objects unless the pronouns actually refer to persons: *met hem* (with him), *tussen ons* (between us), etc. There is nothing in Dutch comparable to the English "with it," "against it," "for it," and the like. In such cases Dutch substitutes *er*, or the more emphatic *daar*, for the pronoun and often makes it a prefix to the preposition:

Dat is een mooi huis. Wonen je vrienden nog *erin*?
That is a beautiful house. Do your friends still live *in it*?

De tafel staat in de woonkamer. De hond slaapt altijd *erop*.
The table is in the living room. The dog always sleeps *on it*.

Daarvoor heb ik niet genoeg geld.
I do not have enough money *for it* (*that*).

Daaraan heb ik al gedacht.   I thought *of that* already.

It is quite common to separate *er/daar* from the preposition:

Hebt u *er* niets *over* gehoord?
Haven't you heard anything *about it*?

Daar heb ik gisteren *van* gelezen.
I read *about that* yesterday.

Ik ben *er* niet aansprakelijk *voor*.
I am not responsible *for it*.

Daar ben ik niet aansprakelijk *voor*.
I am not responsible *for that*.

Daar zijn wij allemaal *mee* tevreden.
We are all satisfied *with that*.

Daar ben ik nog niet *toe* gekomen.
I have not yet come *to that*.

Note that in constructions of this type the prepositions *met* (with) and *tot* (to) become *mee* and *toe*, respectively.

When a question is involved, *er/daar* is replaced by *waar*. Here also, the preposition is frequently separated from its object:

Waaraan denkt hij?   *What* is he thinking *about*?
Waar bent u *mee* tevreden?   *What* are you satisfied *with*?
Waar heb ik te veel *voor*   *What* did I pay too much *for*?
  betald?

The student is advised to review the section on relative pronouns (pp. 42–44) for other uses of prepositional compounds.

TELLING TIME

The most striking difference between the Dutch and English systems of telling time is that Dutch utilizes the half hour as a major point of reference. Whereas English tells time in relation to the hour—the minutes before or after the hour—Dutch employs both the hour and the half hour. The half hour in Dutch is always given as half of the *following* hour. Thus, 4:30 is *half vijf* ("half five"), 7:30 is *half acht*, 10:30 is *half elf*. A quarter past the hour is *kwart over* + the hour; a quarter to the hour is *kwart voor* + the next hour. From a quarter past the hour until a quarter to the next hour Dutch tells time in relation to the half hour. Thus, 1:25 is *vijf voor half twee*, 4:40 is *tien over half vijf*, 5:28 is *twee voor half zes*. The following may serve as a model for the Dutch system of telling time:

2:00	twee uur
2:05	vijf over twee
2:10	tien over twee
2:15	kwart over twee
2:20	tien voor half drie
2:25	vijf voor half drie
2:30	half drie
2:35	vijf over half drie
2:40	tien over half drie
2:45	kwart voor drie
2:50	tien voor drie
2:55	vijf voor drie
3:00	drie uur

When ambiguity might arise, Dutch adds the following qualifiers to the time:

's morgens (OR: 's ochtends)	in the morning
's middags	at noon, in the afternoon
's avonds	in the evening
's nachts	at night

Note also the following expressions:

Hoe laat is het?	What time is it?
Ik heb het kwart over vier.	I have a quarter past four.
Om vijf uur.	*At* five o'clock.
Hij komt *tegen* drie uur.	He's coming *at about* three.

In the Netherlands, as in all of Europe, official time (as for transportation schedules, etc.) uses the 24-hour system. In expressing time in the 24-hour system, the hours past midnight are given first, followed by the number of minutes past the hour. Thus: 7:10 A.M. is *zeven uur tien*, 1:40 P.M. is *dertien* ("thirteen") *uur veertig* and 11:23 P.M. is *drieëntwintig uur drieëntwintig*.

USEFUL EXPRESSIONS

Dag!	Hello! (OR: Bye!)
Goedemorgen.	Good morning.
Goededag.	Good day.
Goedenavond.	Good evening.
Goedenacht.	Good night.
Tot ziens!	So long! (OR: Good-bye!)
Tot straks (OR: Tot kijk).	See you later.
Let op!	Be careful!
Even kijken.	Let's take a look.
Goed zo.	That's fine.
Alles is voor elkaar.	Everything is okay.
Smakelijk eten!	Enjoy your meal!
Welkom in Den Haag.	Welcome to The Hague.
Wel gefeliciteerd!	Congratulations!
Alles goeds.	Best wishes (OR: Good luck).
Veel plezier.	Enjoy yourself (OR: Have a good time).
Welterusten.	Sleep well.
Goede reis!	Have a good trip!
Pardon.	I'm sorry.
Neemt u mij niet kwalijk.	Excuse me.
Wat leuk!	How nice!
Wat jammer!	That's too bad!
Dat mag niet.	That is not allowed.
Dat kan.	That can be done.
Dat hoeft niet.	That isn't necessary.
Het geeft niet.	That's not important.
Dat bevalt me goed.	I like that.
Dat bevalt me niet best.	I don't care for that.
Waar komt u vandaan?	Where are you from?
Hoe maakt u het?	How are you?
Hoe gaat 't met . . . ?	How are things with . . . ?
Heel goed, dank u.	Very well, thank you.

Dank u wel meneer/ mevrouw/juffrouw.	Thank you, sir/madam/miss.
Hartelijk bedankt.	Thanks.
Alstublieft.	Please.
Niet te danken.	Don't mention it.
Tot uw dienst.	At your service.
Het spijt me.	I'm sorry about that.
Ik heet	My name is . . . .
Ik heb honger/dorst.	I am hungry/thirsty.
Ik heb haast.	I'm in a hurry.
Ik heb het erg druk.	I'm very busy.
Ik voel me niet best.	I don't feel too well.
U hebt gelijk.	You are right.
In 't Nederlands/Engels.	In Dutch/English.
Wie is er aan de beurt?	Whose turn is it?
Ik ben er aan de beurt.	It's my turn.
De hoeveelste is 't vandaag?	What is the date today?
Hebt u zin in een kopje koffie?	Would you like a cup of coffee?

IDIOMATIC CONSTRUCTIONS

Idiomatic Expressions Using Common Verbs

There are a number of commonly used verbs in Dutch that merit special attention for the idiomatic constructions in which they occur. The following is a brief sampling of some of the more important of these idiomatic usages:

Doen (to do)

doen als of (to act as though)

Hij doet als of hij dat niet wist.
He acts as though he didn't know that.

doen denken aan (to remind of)

Dat doet me denken aan Piet.   That reminds me of Piet.

dichtdoen (to close)

Ik doe de deur dicht.   I close the door.

opendoen (to open)

Hij doet de deur open.   He opens the door.

pijn doen (to hurt, pain)

Dat doet me pijn.   That hurts me. [That does me pain.]

Gaan (to go)

Hoe gaat het met u?   How are you?
                     [How goes it with you?]
Het gaat me goed.   I am fine. [It goes well for me.]

zitten gaan (to sit down, be seated)

Gaat u even zitten.   Be seated.

Houden (to hold)

houden van (to be fond of, to love)

Hij houdt veel van haar.   He is very fond of her.

Hebben (to have)

> *dorst / honger hebben* (to be thirsty / hungry)

Heb je dorst / honger?   Are you thirsty / hungry?

> *gelijk hebben* (to be right)

Hij heeft gelijk.   He is right.

> *haast hebben* (to be in a hurry)

Ik heb haast.   I am in a hurry.

> *het hebben over* (to talk about)

Zij hebben het over windmolens.
They are talking about windmills.

> *het druk hebben* (to be busy)

Wij hebben het druk op kantoor.
We are busy at the office.

> *het koud / warm hebben* (to be cold / warm)

Ik heb het koud / warm.   I am cold / warm.

> *last hebben van* (to be bothered by)

Wij hadden last van het lawaai.
We were bothered by the noise.
[We had burden from the noise.]

> *nodig hebben* (to need)

Ik heb een auto nodig.   I need a car.
[I have a car necessary.]

> *slaap hebben* (to be sleepy)

Ik heb slaap.   I am sleepy. [I have sleep.]

> *zin hebben in* (to like, to feel like)

Heb je zin in een kopje koffie?
Do you feel like (having) a cup of coffee?

Komen (to come)

Hoe komt het dat . . . ?   How is it that . . . ?

Maken   **(to make, do)**

Hoe maakt u het?   How are you?

[How are you making it?]

Nemen   **(to take)**

kwalijk nemen (to take [something] wrong, to hold against)

Neem me niet kwalijk.   I beg your pardon.

[Don't take me badly.]

Neem het ons niet kwalijk.   Don't hold it against us.

plaats nemen (to sit down)

Neemt u daar plaats.   Sit down over there.

[Take place there.]

Staan   **(to stand)**

Deze hoed staat me niet.   This hat doesn't suit me.

[This hat doesn't stand me.]

Het staat in de krant.   It's in the newspaper.

[It stands in the newspaper.]

Vallen   **(to fall)**

vallen te . . . (one can . . .)

Er valt veel daarover te zeggen.

There is much one can say about that.

[There falls much to say about that.]

meevallen (to turn out well [better than expected])

Het valt vandaag mee met het weer.

Today's weather is better than expected.

tegenvallen (to turn out badly [worse than expected])

Het feest is ons erg tegengevallen.

The festival was a disappointment for us.

Vinden   **(to find)**

plaatsvinden (to take place)

Het heeft al gisteren plaatsgevonden.

It took place yesterday.

Zien   (to see)

er uit zien (to look, to appear)

Zij ziet er vandaag mooi uit.	She looks pretty today.
Het ziet er naar uit dat	It appears that . . . .

Zijn   (to be)

jammer zijn (to be a pity)

Dat is jammer.   That's a pity. [That is misery.]

jarig zijn (to have a birthday)

Hij is morgen jarig.   Tomorrow is his birthday

kwijt zijn (to have lost)

Ik ben mijn sleutels kwijt.   I have lost my keys.

op het punt zijn (to be about to)

Wij zijn op het punt om te vertrekken.
We are about to leave. [We are at the point of leaving.]

van plan zijn (to intend)

Hij is van plan om ons een bezoek te brengen.
He intends to visit us. [He is of plan to bring us a visit.]

voor elkaar zijn (to be in order)

Alles is voor elkaar.
Everything is in order / Everything is fine.

Zitten   (to sit)

De jas zit goed.	The jacket fits well.
	[The jacket sits well.]
Zo zit dat.	That's the way things are. [So sits that.]

Dutch Counterparts of Common English Verbs

Some English verbs convey a wider range of meanings than
any single Dutch verb. In Dutch the ideas conveyed by these
verbs are separated and expressed in two (or more) verbs.

Kennen and weten

The verb "to know" may be rendered in Dutch by either
kennen (kende, gekend) or weten (wist, geweten), depending upon the

specific meaning of the English verb. When general familiarity or knowledge of persons is indicated, the Dutch equivalent is *kennen*; specific knowledge—knowledge or mastery of facts—is expressed by *weten*:

Ik ken deze man, maar ik weet niet waar hij woont.
I know this man, but I don't know where he lives.

Hij kent Amsterdam heel goed.
He knows Amsterdam very well.

Weet je hoeveel het kost?
Do you know how much it costs?

Dat weet ik niet.
I don't know (that).

Leven and *wonen*

When "to live" means "to be alive, to exist, to subsist," it is rendered in Dutch by *leven*; "to live" in the sense "to dwell, to reside" requires the verb *wonen*:

Hij heeft lang geleefd.	He lived a long time.
Zij leven van melk en appels.	They live on milk and apples.
Wij wonen nog in Utrecht.	We still live in Utrecht.

Betekenen and *bedoelen*

The verb "to mean" is rendered in Dutch by *betekenen* when the sense is that of "to signify." When "to mean" is synonymous with "to intend," the Dutch equivalent is *bedoelen*:

Wat betekent dit woord?
What does this word mean [signify]?

Wat bedoel je met die opmerking?
What do you mean by that remark?

Conversely, a Dutch verb may convey a broader range of meanings than one English verb. The following two examples will demonstrate this.

Lenen

Lenen may mean either "to lend" or "to borrow." The specific meaning is almost always clear from the context:

| Hij leent zijn boek aan haar. | He lends his book to her. |
| Zij leent het boek van hem. | She borrows the book from him. |

Leren

Leren may mean either " to teach " or " to learn":

| Ik leer hem zingen. | I teach him to sing. |
| Wij hebben veel van hem geleerd. | We learned much from him. |

Noemen and heten

Finally, the student should note the two verbs **noemen** (to call, to name) and **heten** (to be called, to be named):

| Zij noemde hem naar zijn vader. | She named him after his father. |
| Hij heet Joris. | He is called Joris. |

Appendix A
PARADIGM OF A WEAK VERB

Horen (to hear)

Active Voice

PRESENT: ik hoor, jij hoort (hoor je?),
hij hoort, u hoort
wij (jullie, zij) horen

IMPERATIVE: hoor!, hoort u!

SIMPLE PAST: ik (jij, hij, u) hoorde
wij (jullie, zij) hoorden

FUTURE: ik zal horen, jij zult (zal) horen,
hij zal horen, u zult horen
wij (jullie, zij) zullen horen

CONDITIONAL: ik zou horen, jij zou horen,
hij zou horen, u zou(dt) horen
wij (jullie, zij) zouden horen

PRESENT PERFECT: ik heb gehoord, jij hebt (heb je?)
gehoord, hij heeft gehoord,
u hebt (heeft) gehoord
wij (jullie, zij) hebben gehoord

PAST PERFECT: ik (jij, hij, u) had gehoord
wij (jullie, zij) hadden gehoord

FUTURE PERFECT: ik zal gehoord hebben, jij zult (zal)
gehoord hebben, hij zal gehoord
hebben, u zult gehoord hebben
wij (jullie, zij) zullen gehoord
hebben

CONDITIONAL PERFECT: ik zou gehoord hebben, jij zou gehoord hebben, hij zou gehoord heb-
ben, u zou(dt) gehoord hebben

wij (jullie, zij) zouden
gehoord hebben

Passive Voice

PRESENT: ik word gehoord, jij wordt (word je?)
                     gehoord, hij wordt gehoord,
                     u wordt gehoord
                     wij (jullie, zij) worden gehoord

SIMPLE PAST: ik (jij, hij, u) werd gehoord
                     wij (jullie, zij) werden gehoord

FUTURE: ik zal gehoord worden, jij zult (zal)
                     gehoord worden, hij zal gehoord
                     worden, u zult gehoord worden
                     wij (jullie, zij) zullen gehoord worden

CONDITIONAL: ik zou gehoord worden, jij zou gehoord
                     worden, hij zou gehoord worden,
                     u zou(dt) gehoord worden
                     wij (jullie, zij) zouden gehoord worden

PRESENT PERFECT: ik ben gehoord, jij bent (ben je?)
                     gehoord, hij is gehoord,
                     u bent (is) gehoord
                     wij (jullie, zij) zijn gehoord

PAST PERFECT: ik (jij, hij, u) was gehoord
                     wij (jullie, zij) waren gehoord

FUTURE PERFECT: ik zal gehoord zijn, jij zult (zal)
                     gehoord zijn, hij zal gehoord zijn,
                     u zult gehoord zijn
                     wij (jullie, zij) zullen gehoord zijn

CONDITIONAL PERFECT: ik zou gehoord zijn, jij zou gehoord
                     zijn, hij zou gehoord zijn,
                     u zou(dt) gehoord zijn
                     wij (jullie, zij) zouden gehoord zijn

Appendix B
PARADIGM OF A STRONG VERB

Roepen   (to call)

Active Voice

PRESENT:
ik roep, jij roept (roep je?),
hij roept, u roept
wij (jullie, zij) roepen

IMPERATIVE:
roep!, roept u!

SIMPLE PAST:
ik (jij, hij, u) riep
wij (jullie, zij) riepen

FUTURE:
ik zal roepen, jij zult (zal) roepen,
hij zal roepen, u zult roepen
wij (jullie, zij) zullen roepen

CONDITIONAL:
ik zou roepen, jij zou roepen,
hij zou roepen, u zou(dt) roepen
wij (jullie, zij) zouden roepen

PRESENT PERFECT:
ik heb geroepen, jij hebt (heb je?)
geroepen, hij heeft geroepen,
u hebt (heeft) geroepen
wij (jullie, zij) hebben geroepen

PAST PERFECT:
ik (jij, hij, u) had geroepen
wij (jullie, zij) hadden geroepen

FUTURE PERFECT:
ik zal geroepen hebben,
jij zult (zal) geroepen hebben,
hij zal geroepen hebben,
u zult geroepen hebben
wij (jullie, zij) zullen geroepen hebben

CONDITIONAL PERFECT:
ik zou geroepen hebben, jij zou
geroepen hebben, hij zou geroepen

hebben, u zou(dt) geroepen hebben
wij (jullie, zij) zouden geroepen hebben

Passive Voice

PRESENT:

ik word geroepen, jij wordt (word je?)
geroepen, hij wordt geroepen,
u wordt geroepen
wij (jullie, zij) worden geroepen

SIMPLE PAST:

ik (jij, hij, u) werd geroepen
wij (jullie, zij) werden geroepen

FUTURE:

ik zal geroepen worden,
jij zult (zal) geroepen worden,
hij zal geroepen worden,
u zult geroepen worden
wij (jullie, zij) zullen geroepen worden

CONDITIONAL:

ik zou geroepen worden, jij zou
geroepen worden, hij zou
geroepen worden, u zou(dt)
geroepen worden
wij (jullie, zij) zouden geroepen
worden

PRESENT PERFECT:

ik ben geroepen, jij bent (ben je?)
geroepen, hij is geroepen,
u bent (is) geroepen
wij (jullie, zij) zijn geroepen

PAST PERFECT:

ik (jij, hij, u) was geroepen
wij (jullie, zij) waren geroepen

FUTURE PERFECT:

ik zal geroepen zijn, jij zult (zal)
geroepen zijn, hij zal geroepen zijn,
u zult geroepen zijn
wij (jullie, zij) zullen geroepen zijn

CONDITIONAL PERFECT:

ik zou geroepen zijn, jij zou geroepen
zijn, hij zou geroepen zijn,
u zou(dt) geroepen zijn
wij (jullie, zij) zouden geroepen zijn

Appendix C

PRINCIPAL PARTS OF COMMON STRONG VERBS

The following is a list of the most common strong verbs in Dutch with their principal parts and meaning. For the simple past tense both singular and plural forms have been included to remind the student of variations in spelling. One should note particularly those verbs whose past tense is marked with an asterisk, since their root vowels are short in the singular but long in the plural.

INFINITIVE	SIMPLE PAST	PAST PARTICIPLE	MEANING
beginnen	begon/begonnen	begonnen	to begin
bevelen	*beval/bevalen	bevolen	to order, command
bidden	*bad/baden	gebeden	to pray, entreat
bieden	bood/boden	geboden	to offer
bijten	beet/beten	gebeten	to bite
binden	bond/bonden	gebonden	to tie, bind
blazen	blies/bliezen	geblazen	to blow
blijken	bleek/bleken	gebleken	to be evident, obvious
blijven	bleef/bleven	gebleven	to remain, stay
breken	*brak/braken	gebroken	to break
buigen	boog/bogen	gebogen	to bend
dragen	droeg/droegen	gedragen	to carry, bear
drijven	dreef/dreven	gedreven	to drive, propel
dringen	drong/drongen	gedrongen	to push, press
drinken	dronk/dronken	gedronken	to drink
dwingen	dwong/dwongen	gedwongen	to force, compel
eten	*at/aten	gegeten	to eat
genezen	*genas/genazen	genezen	to cure, heal; to get well
genieten	genoot/genoten	genoten	to enjoy
geven	*gaf/gaven	gegeven	to give
gieten	goot/goten	gegoten	to pour
glijden	gleed/gleden	gegleden	to glide, slide
graven	groef/groeven	gegraven	to dig

INFINITIVE	SIMPLE PAST	PAST PARTICIPLE	MEANING
grijpen	greep/grepen	gegrepen	to catch, grasp
helpen	hielp/hielpen	geholpen	to help
houden	hield/hielden	gehouden	to hold, keep
houwen	hieuw/hieuwen	gehouwen	to cut, hew
kiezen	koos/kozen	gekozen	to choose, select
kijken	keek/keken	gekeken	to look at
klimmen	klom/klommen	geklommen	to climb, ascend
klinken	klonk/klonken	geklonken	to ring, sound
komen	*kwam/kwamen	gekomen	to come
krijgen	kreeg/kregen	gekregen	to get, receive, obtain
kruipen	kroop/kropen	gekropen	to creep, crawl
laten	liet/lieten	gelaten	to allow; to cause; to refrain from
lezen	*las/lazen	gelezen	to read
liegen	loog/logen	gelogen	to tell lies
liggen	*lag/lagen	gelegen	to lie, be situated
lijden	leed/leden	geleden	to suffer, endure
lijken	leek/leken	geleken	to be like; to seem
lopen	liep/liepen	gelopen	to run; to walk
meten	*mat/maten	gemeten	to measure
nemen	*nam/namen	genomen	to take
prijzen	prees/prezen	geprezen	to praise
rijden	reed/reden	gereden	to ride
roepen	riep/riepen	geroepen	to call
schenken	schonk/schonken	geschonken	to pour; to give
schieten	schoot/schoten	geschoten	to shoot
schijnen	scheen/schenen	geschenen	to shine; to seem, appear
schrijven	schreef/schreven	geschreven	to write
schrikken	schrok/schrokken	geschrokken	to be frightened
schuiven	schoof/schoven	geschoven	to push, shove
slaan	sloeg/sloegen	geslagen	to strike, hit
slapen	sliep/sliepen	geslapen	to sleep
sluiten	sloot/sloten	gesloten	to shut, close
snijden	sneed/sneden	gesneden	to cut, carve
spijten	speet/speten	gespeten	to feel sorry (impersonal verb)
spreken	*sprak/spraken	gesproken	to speak
springen	sprong/sprongen	gesprongen	to jump, leap, burst
steken	*stak/staken	gestoken	to sting, stick; to put
stelen	*stal/stalen	gestolen	to steal
sterven	stierf/stierven	gestorven	to die
stijgen	steeg/stegen	gestegen	to climb, rise

INFINITIVE	SIMPLE PAST	PAST PARTICIPLE	MEANING
treffen	trof/troffen	getroffen	to hit, strike; to meet
trekken	trok/trokken	getrokken	to draw, pull;
vallen	viel/vielen	gevallen	to fall
varen	voer/voeren	gevaren	to sail
verdwijnen	verdween/verdwenen	verdwenen	to disappear
vergeten	*vergat/vergaten	vergeten	to forget
verliezen	verloor/verloren	verloren	to lose
vinden	vond/vonden	gevonden	to find
vliegen	vloog/vlogen	gevlogen	to fly
wijken	week/weken	geweken	to yield, give way
winden	wond/wonden	gewonden	to wind, twist
winnen	won/wonnen	gewonnen	to win, gain
worden	werd/werden	geworden	to become
zingen	zong/zongen	gezongen	to sing
zinken	zonk/zonken	gezonken	to sink
zitten	*zat/zaten	gezeten	to sit
zwemmen	zwom/zwommen	gezwommen	to swim
zwijgen	zweeg/zwegen	gezwegen	to be silent; to fall silent

The Seven Classes of Strong Verbs

The following sampling of strong verbs divides them into classes according to their patterns of internal vowel change. It is customary to speak of seven classes of strong verbs in Dutch; note that Classes II, III, V and VI are further subdivided. The strong verb patterns developed in the Germanic languages in prehistoric times. Over the course of centuries they have undergone changes from the combined forces of analogy and leveling. The similarity between Dutch *zingen, zong, gezongen* and English "sing, sang, sung" points to centuries of shared linguistic history; the differences are explained by several centuries of separate development.

INFINITIVE	SIMPLE PAST	PAST PARTICIPLE	MEANING
		Class I	
VOWEL CHANGE **ij**	**ee**	**e**	
bijten	beet	gebeten	to bite
blijven	bleef	gebleven	to remain
glijden	gleed	gegleden	to glide, slide
schrijven	schreef	geschreven	to write

INFINITIVE	SIMPLE PAST	PAST PARTICIPLE	MEANING
		Class II, A	
VOWEL CHANGE ie	oo	o	
gieten	goot	gegoten	to pour
kiezen	koos	gekozen	to choose
schieten	schoot	geschoten	to shoot
vliegen	vloog	gevlogen	to fly
		Class II, B	
VOWEL CHANGE ui	oo	o	
buigen	boog	gebogen	to bend
kruipen	kroop	gekropen	to creep
sluiten	sloot	gesloten	to shut, close
zuigen	zoog	gezogen	to suck
		Class III, A	
VOWEL CHANGE i	o	o	
binden	bond	gebonden	to tie, bind
drinken	dronk	gedronken	to drink
vinden	vond	gevonden	to find
zingen	zong	gezongen	to sing
		Class III, B	
VOWEL CHANGE e	o	o	
bergen	borg	geborgen	to hold, store
schenken	schonk	geschonken	to give, pour
treffen	trof	getroffen	to meet, hit
zwemmen	zwom	gezwommen	to swim
		Class IV	
VOWEL CHANGE e	a	o	
breken	brak	gebroken	to break
nemen	nam	genomen	to take
spreken	sprak	gesproken	to speak
stelen	stal	gestolen	to steal
		Class V, A	
VOWEL CHANGE e	a	e	
eten	at	gegeten	to eat
geven	gaf	gegeven	to give
lezen	las	gelezen	to read
vergeten	vergat	vergeten	to forgive

	INFINITIVE	SIMPLE PAST	PAST PARTICIPLE	MEANING
		Class V, B		
VOWEL CHANGE	i	a	e	
	bidden	bad	gebeden	to pray
	liggen	lag	gelegen	to lie
	zitten	zat	gezeten	to sit
		Class VI, A		
VOWEL CHANGE	(varies)	ie	(varies*)	
	houden	hield	gehouden	to hold
	laten	liet	gelaten	to let, allow
	roepen	riep	geroepen	to call
	vallen	viel	gevallen	to fall
		Class VI, B		
VOWEL CHANGE	e	ie	o	
	helpen	hielp	geholpen	to help
	sterven	stierf	gestorven	to die
		Class VII		
VOWEL CHANGE	a	oe	a	
	dragen	droeg	gedragen	to carry
	graven	groef	gegraven	to dig
	slaan	sloeg	geslagen	to strike
	varen	voer	gevaren	to travel by boat

---

* Coincides with vowel of infinitive.

Appendix D

PRINCIPAL PARTS OF
COMMON IRREGULAR VERBS

The following is a list of the most common irregular verbs in Dutch with their principal parts and meaning.

INFINITIVE	SIMPLE PAST	PAST PARTICIPLE	MEANING
bakken	bakte	gebakken	to bake, fry
barsten	barstte	gebarsten	to burst
brengen	bracht	gebracht	to bring
denken	dacht	gedacht	to think
doen	deed	gedaan	to do
gaan	ging	gegaan	to go
hangen	hing	gehangen	to hang, suspend
hebben	had	gehad	to have
heten	heette	geheten	to be called, be named
kopen	kocht	gekocht	to buy
kunnen	kon	gekund	to be able, can
lachen	lachte	gelachen	to laugh
mogen	mocht	gemoogd	to be allowed to
raden	raadde	geraden	to advise, guess at
scheiden	scheidde	gescheiden	to divide, sever
scheppen	schiep	geschapen	to create
scheren	schoor	geschoren	to shave, shear
staan	stond	gestaan	to stand
stoten	stootte	gestoten	to push, kick
vangen	ving	gevangen	to catch, capture
vragen	vroeg	gevraagd	to ask
vriezen	vroor	gevroren	to freeze
wassen	waste	gewassen	to wash
wegen	woog	gewogen	to weigh, ponder
weten	wist	geweten	to know
willen	wilde	gewild	to want to, wish

INFINITIVE	SIMPLE PAST	PAST PARTICIPLE	MEANING
worden	werd	geworden	to become
zeggen	zei	gezegd	to say, tell
zien	zag	gezien	to see
zijn	was	geweest	to be
zoeken	zocht	gezocht	to seek, look for
zullen	zou	——	shall

The very common verbs *zijn* (to be), *hebben* (to have), and *zullen* (shall, will) are irregular in the present tense as well as in the past. Their forms are repeated here for convenience of review.

	zijn	*hebben*	*zullen*
ik	ben	heb	zal
jij	bent	hebt	zult
hij	is	heeft	zal
u	bent (is)	hebt (heeft)	zult
wij	zijn	hebben	zullen
jullie	zijn	hebben	zullen
zij	zijn	hebben	zullen

The singular and plural forms of the verbs in the past tense are *was/waren, had/hadden,* and *zou/zouden,* respectively.

A GLOSSARY OF GRAMMATICAL TERMS

E. F. Bleiler

This section is intended to refresh your memory of grammatical terms or to clear up difficulties you may have had in understanding them. Before you work through the grammar, you should have a reasonably clear idea what the parts of speech and parts of a sentence are. This is not for reasons of pedantry, but simply because it is easier to talk about grammar if we agree upon terms. Grammatical terminology is as necessary to the study of grammar as the names of automobile parts are to garagemen.

This list is not exhaustive, and the definitions do not pretend to be complete, or to settle points of interpretation that grammarians have been disputing for the past several hundred years. It is a working analysis rather than a scholarly investigation. The definitions given, however, represent most typical American usage, and should serve for basic use.

The Parts of Speech

English words can be divided into eight important groups: nouns, adjectives, articles, verbs, adverbs, pronouns, prepositions, and conjunctions. The boundaries between one group of words and another are sometimes vague and ill-felt in English, but a good dictionary, like the Webster Collegiate, can help you make decisions in questionable cases. Always bear in mind, however, that the way a word is used in a sentence may be just as important as the nature of the word itself in deciding what part of speech the word is.

Nouns. *Nouns* are the *words* for *things* of all *sorts*, whether these *things* are real *objects* that you can see, or *ideas*, or *places*, or *qualities*, or *groups*, or more abstract *things*. *Examples* of *words* that are *nouns* are *cat, vase, door, shrub, wheat, university, mercy, intelligence,*

95

ocean, plumber, pleasure, society, army. If you are in *doubt* whether a given *word* is a *noun*, try putting the *word* "my," or "this," or "large" (or some other *adjective*) in *front* of it. If it makes *sense* in the *sentence* the *chances* are that the *word* in *question* is a *noun.* [All the *words* in *italics* in this *paragraph* are *nouns.*]

Adjectives.   Adjectives are the words which delimit or give you *specific* information about the *various* nouns in a sentence. They tell you size, color, weight, pleasantness, and many *other* qualities. *Such* words as *big, expensive, terrible, insipid, hot, delightful, ruddy, informative* are all *clear* adjectives. If you are in *any* doubt whether a *certain* word is an adjective, add -er to it, or put the word "more" or "too" in front of it. If it makes *good* sense in the sentence, and does not end in -ly, the chances are that it is an adjective. (Pronoun-adjectives will be described under pronouns.) [The adjectives in the *above* sentences are in italics.]

Articles.   There are only two kinds of articles in English, and they are easy to remember. The definite article is "the" and the indefinite article is "a" or "an."

Verbs.   Verbs *are* the words that *tell* what action, or condition, or relationship *is going* on. Such words as *was, is, jumps, achieved, keeps, buys, sells, has finished, run, will have, may, should pay, indicates are* all verb forms. *Observe* that a verb *can be composed* of more than one word, like *will have* and *should pay,* above; these *are called* compound verbs. As a rough guide for verbs, *try adding* -ed to the word you *are wondering* about, or *taking* off an -ed that *is* already there. If it *makes* sense, the chances *are* that it *is* a verb. (This *does* not always *work,* since the so-called strong or irregular verbs *make* forms by *changing* their middle vowels, like *spring, sprang, sprung.*) [Verbs in this paragraph *are* in italics.]

Adverbs.   An adverb is a word that supplies additional information about a verb, an adjective, or another adverb. It *usually* indicates time, or manner, or place, or degree. It tells you *how,* or *when,* or *where,* or to what degree things are happening. Such words as *now, then, there, not, anywhere, never, somehow, always, very,* and most words ending in -ly are *ordinarily* adverbs. [Italicized words are adverbs.]

Pronouns.   Pronouns are related to nouns, and take their place. (Some grammars and dictionaries group pronouns and nouns together as substantives.) *They* mention persons, or objects of any sort without actually giving their names.

There are several different kinds of pronouns. (1) Personal pronouns: by a grammatical convention *I, we, me, mine, us, ours* are called first person pronouns, since *they* refer to the speaker; *you* and *yours* are called second person pronouns, since *they* refer to the person addressed; and *he, him, his, she, her, hers, they, them, theirs* are called third person pronouns since *they* refer to the things or persons discussed. (2) Demonstrative pronouns: *this, that, these, those.* (3) Interrogative, or question, pronouns: *who, whom, what, whose, which.* (4) Relative pronouns, or pronouns *which* refer back to something already mentioned: *who, whom, that, which.* (5) Others: *some, any, anyone, no one, other, whichever, none,* etc.

Pronouns are difficult for *us,* since our categories are not as clear as in some other languages, and *we* use the same words for *what* foreign-language speakers see as different situations. First, our interrogative and relative pronouns overlap, and must be separated in translation. The easiest way is to observe whether a question is involved in the sentence. Examples: " *Which* [int.] do *you* like? " " The inn, *which* [rel.] was not far from Utrecht, had a restaurant." " *Who* [int.] is there? " " *I* don't know *who* [int.] was there." " The porter *who* [rel.] took our bags was Number 2132." *This* may seem to be a trivial difference to an English speaker, but in some languages *it* is very important.

Secondly, there is an overlap between pronouns and adjectives. In some cases the word " this," for example, is a pronoun; in other cases *it* is an adjective. *This* also holds true for *his, its, her, any, none, other, some, that, these, those,* and many other words. Note whether the word in question stands alone or is associated with another word. Examples: " *This* [pronoun] is mine." " This [adj.] taxi has no springs." Watch out for the word " that," which can be a pronoun or an adjective or a conjunction. And remember that " my," " your," " our," and " their " are always adjectives. [All pronouns in this section are in italics.]

Prepositions. Prepositions are the little words that introduce phrases that tell *about* condition, time, place, manner, association, degree, and similar topics. Such words as *with, in, beside, under, of, to, about, for,* and *upon* are prepositions. In English prepositions and adverbs overlap, but, as you will see *by* check-ing *in* your dictionary, there are usually differences *of* meaning *between* the two uses. [Prepositions *in* this paragraph are desig-nated *by* italics.]

Conjunctions. Conjunctions are joining-words. They enable you to link words *or* groups of words into larger units, *and* to build compound *or* complex sentences out of simple sentence units. Such words as *and, but, although, or, unless,* are typical con-junctions. *Although* most conjunctions are easy enough to iden-tify, the word "that" should be watched closely to see *that* it is not a pronoun *or* an adjective. [Conjunctions italicized.]

Words about Verbs

Verbs are responsible for most of the terminology in this short grammar. The basic terms are:

Conjugation. In many languages verbs fall into natural groups, according to the way they make their forms. These groupings are called conjugations, and are an aid to learning grammatical structure. Though it may seem difficult at first to speak of First and Second Conjugations, these are simply short ways of saying that verbs belonging to these classes make their forms according to certain consistent rules, which you can memorize.

Infinitive. This is the basic form which most dictionaries give for verbs in most languages, and in most languages it serves as the basis for classifying verbs. In English (with a very few exceptions) it has no special form. To find the infinitive for any English verb, just fill in this sentence: "I like to . . . (walk, run, jump, swim, carry, disappear, etc.)." The infinitive in English is usually preceded by the word "to." In Dutch infinitives end in *-en* or *-n*.

Tense. This is simply a formal way of saying "time." In English we think of time as being broken into three great seg-ments: past, present, and future. Our verbs are assigned forms to indicate this division, and are further subdivided for shades of meaning. We subdivide the present time into the present (I walk) and present progressive (I am walking); the past into the simple past (I walked), progressive past (I was walking), perfect or present perfect (I have walked), past perfect or pluperfect (I had walked); and future into simple future (I shall walk) and future progressive (I shall be walking). These are the most common English tenses. Dutch tenses are very similar to English ones, except that Dutch does not have progressive tenses.

Present Participles, Progressive Tenses. In English the present participle always ends in -*ing*. It can be used as a noun or an adjective in some situations, but its chief use is in *forming* the so-called progressive tenses. These are made by *putting* appropriate forms of the verb "to be" before a present participle: In "to walk" [an infinitive], for example, the present progressive would be: I am *walking*, you are *walking*, he is *walking*, etc.; past progressive, I was *walking*, you were *walking*, and so on. [Present participles are in italics.]

Past Participles, Perfect Tenses. The past participle in English is not *formed* as regularly as is the present participle. Sometimes it is *constructed* by adding -ed or -d to the present tense, as in *walked, jumped, looked, received*; but there are many verbs where it is *formed* less regularly: *seen, been, swum, chosen, brought*. To find it, simply fill out the sentence "I have . . . ." putting in the verb form that your ear tells you is right for the particular verb. If you speak grammatically, you will have the past participle.

Past participles are sometimes used as adjectives: "Don't cry over *spilt* milk." Their most important use, however, is to form the system of verb tenses that are *called* the perfect tenses: present perfect (or perfect), past perfect (or pluperfect), etc. In English the present perfect tense is *formed* with the present tense of "to have" and the past participle of a verb: I have *walked*, you have *run*, he has *begun*, etc. The past perfect is *formed*, similarly, with the past tense of "to have" and the past participle: I had *walked*, you had *run*, he had *begun*. Most of the languages you are likely to study have similar systems of perfect tenses, though they may not be *formed* in exactly the same way as in English. [Past participles in italics.]

Preterit, Imperfect. Many languages have more than one verb tense for expressing an action that took place in the past. They may use a perfect tense (which we have just covered), or a preterit (simple past), or an imperfect. English, although you may never have thought about it, is one of these languages, for we can say "I have spoken to him" [present perfect], or "I spoke to him" [simple past], or "I was speaking to him" [past progressive]. These sentences do not mean exactly the same thing, although the differences are subtle, and are difficult to put into other words.

While usage differs a little from language to language, if a language has both a preterit and an imperfect, in general the preterit corresponds to the English simple past (I ran, I swam, I spoke), and the imperfect corresponds to the English past progressive (I was running, I was swimming, I was speaking). If you are curious to discover the mode of thought behind these different tenses, try looking at the situation in terms of background-action and point-action. One of the most important uses of the imperfect is to provide a background against which a single point-action can take place. For example, "When I was walking down the street [background, continued over a period of time, hence past progressive or imperfect], I stubbed my toe [an instant or point of time, hence a simple past or preterit]."

Auxiliary Verbs.   Auxiliary verbs are special words that are used to help other verbs make their forms. In English, for example, we use forms of the verb "to have" to make our perfect tenses: I have seen, you had come, he has been, etc. We also use "shall" or "will" to make our future tenses: I shall pay, you will see, etc. Dutch, German, Spanish and Italian also make use of auxiliary verbs, but although the general concept is present, the use of auxiliaries differs from one language to another, and you must learn the practice for each language.

Reflexive.   This term, which sounds more difficult than it really is, simply means that the verb flexes back upon the noun or pronoun that is its subject. In modern English the reflexive pronoun always has -*self* on its end, and we do not use the construction very frequently. In other languages, however, reflexive forms may be used more frequently, and in ways that do not seem very logical to an English speaker. Examples of English reflexive sentences: "He washes himself." "He seated himself at the table."

Passive.   In some languages, like Latin, there is a strong feeling that an action or thing that is taking place can be expressed in two different ways. One can say, A does-something-to B, which is "active"; or B is-having-something-done-to-him by A, which is "passive." We do not have a strong feeling for this' classification of experience in English, but the following examples should indicate the difference between an active and a passive verb: Active: "John is building a house." Passive: "A house is being built by John." Active: "The steamer carried the cotton to England." Passive: "The cotton was carried by the steamer to England." Bear in mind that the formation of passive verbs and the situations where they can be used vary enormously from language to language. This is one situation where you usually cannot translate English word for word into another language and make sense.

Impersonal Verbs. In English there are some verbs which do not have an ordinary subject, and do not refer to persons. They are always used with the pronoun *it*, which does not refer to anything specifically, but simply serves to fill out the verb forms. Examples: It is snowing. It hailed last night. It seems to me that you are wrong. It has been raining. It won't do.

Other languages, like Dutch, have this same general concept, but impersonal verbs may differ quite a bit in form and frequency from one language to another.

Working Verbs. In some languages, English and Dutch, for example, all verb forms *can* be classified into two broad groups: inactive forms and working forms. The inactive verb forms *are* the infinitive, the past participle, and the present participle. All other forms *are* working forms, whether they *are* solitary verbs or parts of compound verbs. All working verbs *share* this characteristic: they *are* modified to show person or time; inactive verbs *are* not changed. Examples: We *have* sixteen dollars. We *left* at four o'clock. We *shall* spend two hours there. The guide *can* pick us up tomorrow. You *are* being paged in the lobby. They *are* now crossing the square. I *have* not decided. [The first two examples *are* solitary verbs; the last five *are* working parts of compound verbs.]

In English this idea *is* not too important. In Dutch, however, it *is* extremely important, since working verbs and inactive forms often *go* in different places in the sentence. [Working verbs *are* placed in italics.]

Words about Nouns

Predicate Nominatives, Predicate Complements, Copulas. The verb "to be" and its forms (am, are, is, was, were, have been, etc.) are sometimes called copulas or copulating verbs, since they couple together elements that are more or less equal. In some languages the words that follow a copula are treated differently than the words that follow other verbs.

In English, an independent adjective (without a noun) that follows a copula is called a predicate adjective or predicate complement, while the nouns or pronouns that follow copulas are called predicate nominatives. In classical English grammar these words are considered (on the model of Latin grammar) to be in the nominative (or subject) case, and therefore we say "It is I" or "It is he." As you can understand, since only a handful of pronouns have a nominative form that is distinguishable from other forms, the English (and Dutch) predicate nominative is a minor point.

Gender. Gender should not be confused with actual sex. In many languages nouns are arbitrarily assigned a gender (masculine or feminine, or common or neuter), and this need not correspond to sex. You simply have to learn the pattern of the language you are studying in order to become familiar with its use of gender.

Case. The idea of case is often very difficult for an English-speaker to grasp, since we do not use case very much. Perhaps the best way to understand how case works is to step behind words themselves, into the ideas which words express. If you look at a sentence like "Mr. Brown is paying the waiter," you can see that three basic ideas are involved: Mr. Brown, the waiter, and the act of payment. The problem that every language has is to show how these ideas are to be related, or how words are to be interlocked to form sentences.

Surprisingly enough, there are only three ways of putting pointers on words to make your meaning clear, so that your listener knows who is doing what to whom. These ways are (1) word order (2) additional words (3) alteration of the word (which for nouns, pronouns, and adjectives is called case).

Word order, or the place of individual words in a sentence, is very important in English. For us, "Mr. Brown is paying the waiter" is entirely different in meaning from "The waiter is paying Mr. Brown." This may seem so obvious that it need not be mentioned, but in some languages, like Latin, you can shift the positions of the words and come out with the same meaning for the sentence, apart from shifts of emphasis.

Adding other elements, to make meanings clear, is also commonly used in English. We have a whole range of words like "to, from, with, in, out, of," and so on, which show relationships. "Mr. Jones introduced Mr. Smith to the Captain" is unambiguous because of the word " to."

Altering the word itself is called case when it is done with nouns, pronouns, or adjectives Most of the time these alterations consist of endings that you place on the word or on its stem. Case endings in nouns thus correspond to the endings that you add to verbs to show time or the speaker. Examples of verb endings: I walk. He walk*s*. We walk*ed*.

Case is not as important in English or Dutch as it is in some languages, but both languages do use case in a few limited forms. We add an -'s to nouns to form a possessive; we add a similar -s to form the plural for most nouns; and we add (in spelling, though there is no sound change involved) an -' to indicate a possessive plural. In pronouns, sometimes we add endings, as in the words who, whose and whom. Sometimes we use different forms, as in " I, mine, me "; " he, his, him "; " we, ours " and " us."

When you use case, as you can see, you know much more about individual words than if you do not have case. When you see the word "whom" you automatically recognize that it cannot be the subject of a sentence, but must be the object of a verb or a preposition. When you see the word "ship's," you know that it means belonging to a ship or originating from a ship.

Miscellaneous Terms

Comparative, Superlative. These two terms are used with adjectives and adverbs. They indicate the degree of strength within the meaning of the word. Faster, better, earlier, newer, more rapid, more detailed, more suitable are examples of the comparative in adjectives, while more rapidly, more recently, more suitably are comparatives for adverbs. In most cases, as you have seen, the comparative uses -er or "more" for an adjective, and "more" for an adverb. Superlatives are those forms which end in -est or have "most" prefixed before them for adjectives, and "most" prefixed for adverbs: most intelligent, earliest, most rapidly, most suitably.

Idiom. An idiom is an expression that is peculiar to a language, the meaning of which is not the same as the literal meaning of the individual words composing it. Idioms, as a rule, cannot be translated word by word into another language. Examples of English idioms: " *Take it easy.*" "Don't *beat around the bush.*" " It *turned out* to be *a Dutch treat.*" " Can you *tell time* in Spanish?"

The Parts of the Sentence

Subject, Predicate. In grammar *every complete sentence* contains two basic parts, the subject and the predicate. *The subject, if we* state the terms most simply, is the thing, person, or activity talked about. *It* can be a noun, a pronoun, or something *that* serves as a noun. *A subject* would include, in a typical case, a noun, the articles or adjectives *which* are associated with it, and perhaps phrases. Note that in complex sentences, *each part* may have its own subject. [*The subjects of the sentences above* have been italicized.]

The predicate *talks about the subject.* In a formal sentence the predicate *includes a verb, its adverbs, predicate adjectives, phrases, and objects*—whatever *happens to be present.* A predicate adjective *is an adjective* which *happens to be in the predicate after a form of the verb to be.* Example: "Apples *are red.*" [Predicates *are in italics.*]

In the following simple sentences subjects are in italics, predicates in italics and underlined. " *Green apples are bad for your digestion.*" "When *I go to Spain, I always stop in Cadiz.*" " *The man with the handbag is traveling to Delft.*"

Direct and Indirect Objects. Some verbs (called transitive verbs) take direct and/or indirect objects in their predicates; other verbs (called intransitive verbs) do not take objects of any sort. In English, except for pronouns, objects do not have any special forms, but in languages which have case forms or more pronoun forms than English, objects can be troublesome.

The direct object is the person, thing, quality, or matter that the verb directs *its action* upon. It can be a pronoun, or a noun, perhaps accompanied by an article and/or adjectives. In English, the direct object always directly follows *its verb*, except when there is also an indirect object present, which comes between the verb and the object. Prepositions do not go before direct objects. Examples: " The cook threw *green onions* into the stew." " The border guards will want to see *your passport* tomorrow." " Give *it* to me." " Please give me *a glass of red wine*." [We have placed *direct objects* in this paragraph in italics.]

The indirect object, as grammars will tell *you*, is the person or thing for or to whom the action is taking place. It can be a pronoun or a noun with or without article and adjectives. In most cases the words " to " or " for " can be inserted before it, if not already there. Examples: " Please tell *me* the time." " I wrote *her* a letter from Barcelona." " We sent *Mr. Gonzalez* ten pesos." " We gave *the most energetic guide* a large tip." [Indirect objects are in italics.]

Clauses: Independent, Dependent, Relative. Clauses are the largest components / *that go to make up sentences.* / Each clause, in classical grammar, is a combination of subject and predicate. / *If a sentence has one subject and one predicate,* / it is a one-clause sentence. / *If it has two or more subjects and predicates,* / it is a sentence of two or more clauses. /

There are two kinds of clauses: independent (principal) and dependent (subordinate) clauses. / An independent clause can stand alone; / it can form a logical, complete sentence. / A dependent clause is a clause / *that cannot stand alone*; / it must have another clause with it to complete it. /

A sentence containing a single clause is called a simple sentence. / A sentence with two or more clauses may be either a complex or a compound sentence. / A compound sentence contains two or more independent clauses, / and / these independent clauses are joined together with " and " or " but," / *which are known as coordinating conjunctions.* / A complex sentence is a sentence / *which contains both independent and dependent clauses.* /

A relative clause is a clause / *which begins with a relative pronoun: who, whom, that, which.* / It is by definition a dependent clause, / *since it cannot stand by itself.* Other dependent (subordinate) clauses are introduced by subordinating conjunctions, such as "although," "because," or "in order that." (Dutch subordinating conjunctions and rules for their usage may be found on p. 69–70.)

In English these terms are not very important except for rhetorical analysis, / *since all clauses are treated very much the same in grammar and syntax.* In some foreign languages like Dutch, however, these concepts are important, / and they must be understood, / *since all clauses are not treated alike.* [Each clause in this section has been isolated by slashes. / Dependent clauses have been placed in italics; / independent clauses have not been marked. /]

INDEX

The abbreviation *def.* has been used in this index for definition. Dutch words appear in *italic* and their English equivalents in parentheses.

A CATALOG OF SELECTED
DOVER BOOKS
IN ALL FIELDS OF INTEREST

A CATALOG OF SELECTED DOVER
BOOKS IN ALL FIELDS OF INTEREST

CONCERNING THE SPIRITUAL IN ART, Wassily Kandinsky. Pioneering work by father of abstract art. Thoughts on color theory, nature of art. Analysis of earlier masters. 12 illustrations. 80pp. of text. 5⅜ x 8½. 23411-8

ANIMALS: 1,419 Copyright-Free Illustrations of Mammals, Birds, Fish, Insects, etc., Jim Harter (ed.). Clear wood engravings present, in extremely lifelike poses, over 1,000 species of animals. One of the most extensive pictorial sourcebooks of its kind. Captions. Index. 284pp. 9 x 12. 23766-4

CELTIC ART: The Methods of Construction, George Bain. Simple geometric techniques for making Celtic interlacements, spirals, Kells-type initials, animals, humans, etc. Over 500 illustrations. 160pp. 9 x 12. (Available in U.S. only.) 22923-8

AN ATLAS OF ANATOMY FOR ARTISTS, Fritz Schider. Most thorough reference work on art anatomy in the world. Hundreds of illustrations, including selections from works by Vesalius, Leonardo, Goya, Ingres, Michelangelo, others. 593 illustrations. 192pp. 7⅛ x 10¼. 20241-0

CELTIC HAND STROKE-BY-STROKE (Irish Half-Uncial from "The Book of Kells"): An Arthur Baker Calligraphy Manual, Arthur Baker. Complete guide to creating each letter of the alphabet in distinctive Celtic manner. Covers hand position, strokes, pens, inks, paper, more. Illustrated. 48pp. 8¼ x 11. 24336-2

EASY ORIGAMI, John Montroll. Charming collection of 32 projects (hat, cup, pelican, piano, swan, many more) specially designed for the novice origami hobbyist. Clearly illustrated easy-to-follow instructions insure that even beginning papercrafters will achieve successful results. 48pp. 8¼ x 11. 27298-2

THE COMPLETE BOOK OF BIRDHOUSE CONSTRUCTION FOR WOODWORKERS, Scott D. Campbell. Detailed instructions, illustrations, tables. Also data on bird habitat and instinct patterns. Bibliography. 3 tables. 63 illustrations in 15 figures. 48pp. 5¼ x 8½. 24407-5

BLOOMINGDALE'S ILLUSTRATED 1886 CATALOG: Fashions, Dry Goods and Housewares, Bloomingdale Brothers. Famed merchants' extremely rare catalog depicting about 1,700 products: clothing, housewares, firearms, dry goods, jewelry, more. Invaluable for dating, identifying vintage items. Also, copyright-free graphics for artists, designers. Co-published with Henry Ford Museum & Greenfield Village. 160pp. 8¼ x 11. 25780-0

HISTORIC COSTUME IN PICTURES, Braun & Schneider. Over 1,450 costumed figures in clearly detailed engravings—from dawn of civilization to end of 19th century. Captions. Many folk costumes. 256pp. 8⅜ x 11¾. 23150-X

STICKLEY CRAFTSMAN FURNITURE CATALOGS, Gustav Stickley and L. & J. G. Stickley. Beautiful, functional furniture in two authentic catalogs from 1910. 594 illustrations, including 277 photos, show settles, rockers, armchairs, reclining chairs, bookcases, desks, tables. 183pp. 6½ x 9¼. 23838-5

AMERICAN LOCOMOTIVES IN HISTORIC PHOTOGRAPHS: 1858 to 1949, Ron Ziel (ed.). A rare collection of 126 meticulously detailed official photographs, called "builder portraits," of American locomotives that majestically chronicle the rise of steam locomotive power in America. Introduction. Detailed captions. xi+ 129pp. 9 x 12. 27393-8

AMERICA'S LIGHTHOUSES: An Illustrated History, Francis Ross Holland, Jr. Delightfully written, profusely illustrated fact-filled survey of over 200 American lighthouses since 1716. History, anecdotes, technological advances, more. 240pp. 8 x 10¾. 25576-X

TOWARDS A NEW ARCHITECTURE, Le Corbusier. Pioneering manifesto by founder of "International School." Technical and aesthetic theories, views of industry, economics, relation of form to function, "mass-production split" and much more. Profusely illustrated. 320pp. 6⅛ x 9¼. (Available in U.S. only.) 25023-7

HOW THE OTHER HALF LIVES, Jacob Riis. Famous journalistic record, exposing poverty and degradation of New York slums around 1900, by major social reformer. 100 striking and influential photographs. 233pp. 10 x 7⅞. 22012-5

FRUIT KEY AND TWIG KEY TO TREES AND SHRUBS, William M. Harlow. One of the handiest and most widely used identification aids. Fruit key covers 120 deciduous and evergreen species; twig key 160 deciduous species. Easily used. Over 300 photographs. 126pp. 5⅜ x 8½. 20511-8

COMMON BIRD SONGS, Dr. Donald J. Borror. Songs of 60 most common U.S. birds: robins, sparrows, cardinals, bluejays, finches, more—arranged in order of increasing complexity. Up to 9 variations of songs of each species.
Cassette and manual 99911-4

ORCHIDS AS HOUSE PLANTS, Rebecca Tyson Northen. Grow cattleyas and many other kinds of orchids—in a window, in a case, or under artificial light. 63 illustrations. 148pp. 5⅜ x 8½. 23261-1

MONSTER MAZES, Dave Phillips. Masterful mazes at four levels of difficulty. Avoid deadly perils and evil creatures to find magical treasures. Solutions for all 32 exciting illustrated puzzles. 48pp. 8¼ x 11. 26005-4

MOZART'S DON GIOVANNI (DOVER OPERA LIBRETTO SERIES), Wolfgang Amadeus Mozart. Introduced and translated by Ellen H. Bleiler. Standard Italian libretto, with complete English translation. Convenient and thoroughly portable—an ideal companion for reading along with a recording or the performance itself. Introduction. List of characters. Plot summary. 121pp. 5¼ x 8½. 24944-1

TECHNICAL MANUAL AND DICTIONARY OF CLASSICAL BALLET, Gail Grant. Defines, explains, comments on steps, movements, poses and concepts. 15-page pictorial section. Basic book for student, viewer. 127pp. 5⅜ x 8½. 21843-0

THE CLARINET AND CLARINET PLAYING, David Pino. Lively, comprehensive work features suggestions about technique, musicianship, and musical interpretation, as well as guidelines for teaching, making your own reeds, and preparing for public performance. Includes an intriguing look at clarinet history. "A godsend," *The Clarinet,* Journal of the International Clarinet Society. Appendixes. 7 illus. 320pp. 5⅜ x 8½. 40270-3

THE ANNOTATED CASEY AT THE BAT: A Collection of Ballads about the Mighty Casey/Third, Revised Edition, Martin Gardner (ed.). Amusing sequels and parodies of one of America's best-loved poems: Casey's Revenge, Why Casey Whiffed, Casey's Sister at the Bat, others. 256pp. 5⅜ x 8½. 28598-7

THE RAVEN AND OTHER FAVORITE POEMS, Edgar Allan Poe. Over 40 of the author's most memorable poems: "The Bells," "Ulalume," "Israfel," "To Helen," "The Conqueror Worm," "Eldorado," "Annabel Lee," many more. Alphabetic lists of titles and first lines. 64pp. 5$\frac{3}{16}$ x 8¼. 26685-0

PERSONAL MEMOIRS OF U. S. GRANT, Ulysses Simpson Grant. Intelligent, deeply moving firsthand account of Civil War campaigns, considered by many the finest military memoirs ever written. Includes letters, historic photographs, maps and more. 528pp. 6⅛ x 9¼. 28587-1

ANCIENT EGYPTIAN MATERIALS AND INDUSTRIES, A. Lucas and J. Harris. Fascinating, comprehensive, thoroughly documented text describes this ancient civilization's vast resources and the processes that incorporated them in daily life, including the use of animal products, building materials, cosmetics, perfumes and incense, fibers, glazed ware, glass and its manufacture, materials used in the mummification process, and much more. 544pp. 6⅛ x 9¼. (Available in U.S. only.) 40446-3

RUSSIAN STORIES/RUSSKIE RASSKAZY: A Dual-Language Book, edited by Gleb Struve. Twelve tales by such masters as Chekhov, Tolstoy, Dostoevsky, Pushkin, others. Excellent word-for-word English translations on facing pages, plus teaching and study aids, Russian/English vocabulary, biographical/critical introductions, more. 416pp. 5⅜ x 8½. 26244-8

PHILADELPHIA THEN AND NOW: 60 Sites Photographed in the Past and Present, Kenneth Finkel and Susan Oyama. Rare photographs of City Hall, Logan Square, Independence Hall, Betsy Ross House, other landmarks juxtaposed with contemporary views. Captures changing face of historic city. Introduction. Captions. 128pp. 8¼ x 11. 25790-8

AIA ARCHITECTURAL GUIDE TO NASSAU AND SUFFOLK COUNTIES, LONG ISLAND, The American Institute of Architects, Long Island Chapter, and the Society for the Preservation of Long Island Antiquities. Comprehensive, well-researched and generously illustrated volume brings to life over three centuries of Long Island's great architectural heritage. More than 240 photographs with authoritative, extensively detailed captions. 176pp. 8¼ x 11. 26946-9

NORTH AMERICAN INDIAN LIFE: Customs and Traditions of 23 Tribes, Elsie Clews Parsons (ed.). 27 fictionalized essays by noted anthropologists examine religion, customs, government, additional facets of life among the Winnebago, Crow, Zuni, Eskimo, other tribes. 480pp. 6⅛ x 9¼. 27377-6

CATALOG OF DOVER BOOKS

HOLLYWOOD GLAMOR PORTRAITS, John Kobal (ed.). 145 photos from 1926-49. Harlow, Gable, Bogart, Bacall; 94 stars in all. Full background on photographers, technical aspects. 160pp. 8⅜ x 11¼. 23352-9

FRANK LLOYD WRIGHT'S DANA HOUSE, Donald Hoffmann. Pictorial essay of residential masterpiece with over 160 interior and exterior photos, plans, elevations, sketches and studies. 128pp. 9¼ x 10¾. 29120-0

THE MALE AND FEMALE FIGURE IN MOTION: 60 Classic Photographic Sequences, Eadweard Muybridge. 60 true-action photographs of men and women walking, running, climbing, bending, turning, etc., reproduced from rare 19th-century masterpiece. vi + 121pp. 9 x 12. 24745-7

1001 QUESTIONS ANSWERED ABOUT THE SEASHORE, N. J. Berrill and Jacquelyn Berrill. Queries answered about dolphins, sea snails, sponges, starfish, fishes, shore birds, many others. Covers appearance, breeding, growth, feeding, much more. 305pp. 5¼ x 8¼. 23366-9

ATTRACTING BIRDS TO YOUR YARD, William J. Weber. Easy-to-follow guide offers advice on how to attract the greatest diversity of birds: birdhouses, feeders, water and waterers, much more. 96pp. 5³⁄₁₆ x 8¼. 28927-3

MEDICINAL AND OTHER USES OF NORTH AMERICAN PLANTS: A Historical Survey with Special Reference to the Eastern Indian Tribes, Charlotte Erichsen-Brown. Chronological historical citations document 500 years of usage of plants, trees, shrubs native to eastern Canada, northeastern U.S. Also complete identifying information. 343 illustrations. 544pp. 6½ x 9¼. 25951-X

STORYBOOK MAZES, Dave Phillips. 23 stories and mazes on two-page spreads: Wizard of Oz, Treasure Island, Robin Hood, etc. Solutions. 64pp. 8¼ x 11. 23628-5

AMERICAN NEGRO SONGS: 230 Folk Songs and Spirituals, Religious and Secular, John W. Work. This authoritative study traces the African influences of songs sung and played by black Americans at work, in church, and as entertainment. The author discusses the lyric significance of such songs as "Swing Low, Sweet Chariot," "John Henry," and others and offers the words and music for 230 songs. Bibliography. Index of Song Titles. 272pp. 6½ x 9¼. 40271-1

MOVIE-STAR PORTRAITS OF THE FORTIES, John Kobal (ed.). 163 glamor, studio photos of 106 stars of the 1940s: Rita Hayworth, Ava Gardner, Marlon Brando, Clark Gable, many more. 176pp. 8⅜ x 11¼. 23546-7

BENCHLEY LOST AND FOUND, Robert Benchley. Finest humor from early 30s, about pet peeves, child psychologists, post office and others. Mostly unavailable elsewhere. 73 illustrations by Peter Arno and others. 183pp. 5⅜ x 8½. 22410-4

YEKL and THE IMPORTED BRIDEGROOM AND OTHER STORIES OF YIDDISH NEW YORK, Abraham Cahan. Film Hester Street based on *Yekl* (1896). Novel, other stories among first about Jewish immigrants on N.Y.'s East Side. 240pp. 5⅜ x 8½. 22427-9

SELECTED POEMS, Walt Whitman. Generous sampling from *Leaves of Grass*. Twenty-four poems include "I Hear America Singing," "Song of the Open Road," "I Sing the Body Electric," "When Lilacs Last in the Dooryard Bloom'd," "O Captain! My Captain!"—all reprinted from an authoritative edition. Lists of titles and first lines. 128pp. 5³⁄₁₆ x 8¼. 26878-0

PHOTOGRAPHIC SKETCHBOOK OF THE CIVIL WAR, Alexander Gardner. 100 photos taken on field during the Civil War. Famous shots of Manassas Harper's Ferry, Lincoln, Richmond, slave pens, etc. 244pp. 10⅝ x 8¼.   22731-6

FIVE ACRES AND INDEPENDENCE, Maurice G. Kains. Great back-to-the-land classic explains basics of self-sufficient farming. The one book to get. 95 illustrations. 397pp. 5⅜ x 8½.   20974-1

SONGS OF EASTERN BIRDS, Dr. Donald J. Borror. Songs and calls of 60 species most common to eastern U.S.: warblers, woodpeckers, flycatchers, thrushes, larks, many more in high-quality recording.   Cassette and manual 99912-2

A MODERN HERBAL, Margaret Grieve. Much the fullest, most exact, most useful compilation of herbal material. Gigantic alphabetical encyclopedia, from aconite to zedoary, gives botanical information, medical properties, folklore, economic uses, much else. Indispensable to serious reader. 161 illustrations. 888pp. 6½ x 9¼. 2-vol. set. (Available in U.S. only.)   Vol. I: 22798-7
          Vol. II: 22799-5

HIDDEN TREASURE MAZE BOOK, Dave Phillips. Solve 34 challenging mazes accompanied by heroic tales of adventure. Evil dragons, people-eating plants, bloodthirsty giants, many more dangerous adversaries lurk at every twist and turn. 34 mazes, stories, solutions. 48pp. 8¼ x 11.   24566-7

LETTERS OF W. A. MOZART, Wolfgang A. Mozart. Remarkable letters show bawdy wit, humor, imagination, musical insights, contemporary musical world; includes some letters from Leopold Mozart. 276pp. 5⅜ x 8½.   22859-2

BASIC PRINCIPLES OF CLASSICAL BALLET, Agrippina Vaganova. Great Russian theoretician, teacher explains methods for teaching classical ballet. 118 illustrations. 175pp. 5⅜ x 8½.   22036-2

THE JUMPING FROG, Mark Twain. Revenge edition. The original story of The Celebrated Jumping Frog of Calaveras County, a hapless French translation, and Twain's hilarious "retranslation" from the French. 12 illustrations. 66pp. 5⅜ x 8½.   22686-7

BEST REMEMBERED POEMS, Martin Gardner (ed.). The 126 poems in this superb collection of 19th- and 20th-century British and American verse range from Shelley's "To a Skylark" to the impassioned "Renascence" of Edna St. Vincent Millay and to Edward Lear's whimsical "The Owl and the Pussycat." 224pp. 5⅜ x 8½.   27165-X

COMPLETE SONNETS, William Shakespeare. Over 150 exquisite poems deal with love, friendship, the tyranny of time, beauty's evanescence, death and other themes in language of remarkable power, precision and beauty. Glossary of archaic terms. 80pp. 5³⁄₁₆ x 8¼.   26686-9

THE BATTLES THAT CHANGED HISTORY, Fletcher Pratt. Eminent historian profiles 16 crucial conflicts, ancient to modern, that changed the course of civilization. 352pp. 5⅜ x 8½.   41129-X

THE WIT AND HUMOR OF OSCAR WILDE, Alvin Redman (ed.). More than 1,000 ripostes, paradoxes, wisecracks: Work is the curse of the drinking classes; I can resist everything except temptation; etc. 258pp. 5⅜ x 8½. 20602-5

SHAKESPEARE LEXICON AND QUOTATION DICTIONARY, Alexander Schmidt. Full definitions, locations, shades of meaning in every word in plays and poems. More than 50,000 exact quotations. 1,485pp. 6½ x 9¼. 2-vol. set.
Vol. 1: 22726-X
Vol. 2: 22727-8

SELECTED POEMS, Emily Dickinson. Over 100 best-known, best-loved poems by one of America's foremost poets, reprinted from authoritative early editions. No comparable edition at this price. Index of first lines. 64pp. 5³⁄₁₆ x 8¼. 26466-1

THE INSIDIOUS DR. FU-MANCHU, Sax Rohmer. The first of the popular mystery series introduces a pair of English detectives to their archnemesis, the diabolical Dr. Fu-Manchu. Flavorful atmosphere, fast-paced action, and colorful characters enliven this classic of the genre. 208pp. 5³⁄₁₆ x 8¼. 29898-1

THE MALLEUS MALEFICARUM OF KRAMER AND SPRENGER, translated by Montague Summers. Full text of most important witchhunter's "bible," used by both Catholics and Protestants. 278pp. 6⅝ x 10. 22802-9

SPANISH STORIES/CUENTOS ESPAÑOLES: A Dual-Language Book, Angel Flores (ed.). Unique format offers 13 great stories in Spanish by Cervantes, Borges, others. Faithful English translations on facing pages. 352pp. 5⅜ x 8½. 25399-6

GARDEN CITY, LONG ISLAND, IN EARLY PHOTOGRAPHS, 1869–1919, Mildred H. Smith. Handsome treasury of 118 vintage pictures, accompanied by carefully researched captions, document the Garden City Hotel fire (1899), the Vanderbilt Cup Race (1908), the first airmail flight departing from the Nassau Boulevard Aerodrome (1911), and much more. 96pp. 8⅞ x 11¾. 40669-5

OLD QUEENS, N.Y., IN EARLY PHOTOGRAPHS, Vincent F. Seyfried and William Asadorian. Over 160 rare photographs of Maspeth, Jamaica, Jackson Heights, and other areas. Vintage views of DeWitt Clinton mansion, 1939 World's Fair and more. Captions. 192pp. 8⅞ x 11. 26358-4

CAPTURED BY THE INDIANS: 15 Firsthand Accounts, 1750-1870, Frederick Drimmer. Astounding true historical accounts of grisly torture, bloody conflicts, relentless pursuits, miraculous escapes and more, by people who lived to tell the tale. 384pp. 5⅜ x 8½. 24901-8

THE WORLD'S GREAT SPEECHES (Fourth Enlarged Edition), Lewis Copeland, Lawrence W. Lamm, and Stephen J. McKenna. Nearly 300 speeches provide public speakers with a wealth of updated quotes and inspiration–from Pericles' funeral oration and William Jennings Bryan's "Cross of Gold Speech" to Malcolm X's powerful words on the Black Revolution and Earl of Spenser's tribute to his sister, Diana, Princess of Wales. 944pp. 5⅜ x 8⅜. 40903-1

THE BOOK OF THE SWORD, Sir Richard F. Burton. Great Victorian scholar/adventurer's eloquent, erudite history of the "queen of weapons"–from prehistory to early Roman Empire. Evolution and development of early swords, variations (sabre, broadsword, cutlass, scimitar, etc.), much more. 336pp. 6⅛ x 9¼. 25434-8

AUTOBIOGRAPHY: The Story of My Experiments with Truth, Mohandas K. Gandhi. Boyhood, legal studies, purification, the growth of the Satyagraha (nonviolent protest) movement. Critical, inspiring work of the man responsible for the freedom of India. 480pp. 5⅜ x 8½. (Available in U.S. only.) 24593-4

CELTIC MYTHS AND LEGENDS, T. W. Rolleston. Masterful retelling of Irish and Welsh stories and tales. Cuchulain, King Arthur, Deirdre, the Grail, many more. First paperback edition. 58 full-page illustrations. 512pp. 5⅜ x 8½. 26507-2

THE PRINCIPLES OF PSYCHOLOGY, William James. Famous long course complete, unabridged. Stream of thought, time perception, memory, experimental methods; great work decades ahead of its time. 94 figures. 1,391pp. 5⅜ x 8½. 2-vol. set.
Vol. I: 20381-6 Vol. II: 20382-4

THE WORLD AS WILL AND REPRESENTATION, Arthur Schopenhauer. Definitive English translation of Schopenhauer's life work, correcting more than 1,000 errors, omissions in earlier translations. Translated by E. F. J. Payne. Total of 1,269pp. 5⅜ x 8½. 2-vol. set.
Vol. 1: 21761-2 Vol. 2: 21762-0

MAGIC AND MYSTERY IN TIBET, Madame Alexandra David-Neel. Experiences among lamas, magicians, sages, sorcerers, Bonpa wizards. A true psychic discovery. 32 illustrations. 321pp. 5⅜ x 8½. (Available in U.S. only.) 22682-4

THE EGYPTIAN BOOK OF THE DEAD, E. A. Wallis Budge. Complete reproduction of Ani's papyrus, finest ever found. Full hieroglyphic text, interlinear transliteration, word-for-word translation, smooth translation. 533pp. 6½ x 9¼. 21866-X

MATHEMATICS FOR THE NONMATHEMATICIAN, Morris Kline. Detailed, college-level treatment of mathematics in cultural and historical context, with numerous exercises. Recommended Reading Lists. Tables. Numerous figures. 641pp. 5⅜ x 8½.
24823-2

PROBABILISTIC METHODS IN THE THEORY OF STRUCTURES, Isaac Elishakoff. Well-written introduction covers the elements of the theory of probability from two or more random variables, the reliability of such multivariable structures, the theory of random function, Monte Carlo methods of treating problems incapable of exact solution, and more. Examples. 502pp. 5⅜ x 8½. 40691-1

THE RIME OF THE ANCIENT MARINER, Gustave Doré, S. T. Coleridge. Doré's finest work; 34 plates capture moods, subtleties of poem. Flawless full-size reproductions printed on facing pages with authoritative text of poem. "Beautiful. Simply beautiful."–Publisher's Weekly. 77pp. 9¼ x 12. 22305-1

NORTH AMERICAN INDIAN DESIGNS FOR ARTISTS AND CRAFTSPEOPLE, Eva Wilson. Over 360 authentic copyright-free designs adapted from Navajo blankets, Hopi pottery, Sioux buffalo hides, more. Geometrics, symbolic figures, plant and animal motifs, etc. 128pp. 8⅜ x 11. (Not for sale in the United Kingdom.) 25341-4

SCULPTURE: Principles and Practice, Louis Slobodkin. Step-by-step approach to clay, plaster, metals, stone; classical and modern. 253 drawings, photos. 255pp. 8⅛ x 11.
22960-2

THE INFLUENCE OF SEA POWER UPON HISTORY, 1660–1783, A. T. Mahan. Influential classic of naval history and tactics still used as text in war colleges. First paperback edition. 4 maps. 24 battle plans. 640pp. 5⅜ x 8½. 25509-3

CATALOG OF DOVER BOOKS

THE STORY OF THE TITANIC AS TOLD BY ITS SURVIVORS, Jack Winocour (ed.). What it was really like. Panic, despair, shocking inefficiency, and a little hero-ism. More thrilling than any fictional account. 26 illustrations. 320pp. 5⅜ x 8½.
20610-6

FAIRY AND FOLK TALES OF THE IRISH PEASANTRY, William Butler Yeats (ed.). Treasury of 64 tales from the twilight world of Celtic myth and legend: "The Soul Cages," "The Kildare Pooka," "King O'Toole and his Goose," many more. Introduction and Notes by W. B. Yeats. 352pp. 5⅜ x 8½. 26941-8

BUDDHIST MAHAYANA TEXTS, E. B. Cowell and others (eds.). Superb, accurate translations of basic documents in Mahayana Buddhism, highly important in history of religions. The Buddha-karita of Asvaghosha, Larger Sukhavativyuha, more. 448pp. 5⅜ x 8½. 25552-2

ONE TWO THREE . . . INFINITY: Facts and Speculations of Science, George Gamow. Great physicist's fascinating, readable overview of contemporary science: number theory, relativity, fourth dimension, entropy, genes, atomic structure, much more. 128 illustrations. Index. 352pp. 5⅜ x 8½. 25664-2

EXPERIMENTATION AND MEASUREMENT, W. J. Youden. Introductory manual explains laws of measurement in simple terms and offers tips for achieving accuracy and minimizing errors. Mathematics of measurement, use of instruments, experimenting with machines. 1994 edition. Foreword. Preface. Introduction. Epilogue. Selected Readings. Glossary. Index. Tables and figures. 128pp. 5⅜ x 8½.
40451-X

DALÍ ON MODERN ART: The Cuckolds of Antiquated Modern Art, Salvador Dalí. Influential painter skewers modern art and its practitioners. Outrageous evaluations of Picasso, Cézanne, Turner, more. 15 renderings of paintings discussed. 44 calligraphic decorations by Dalí. 96pp. 5⅜ x 8½. (Available in U.S. only.) 29220-7

ANTIQUE PLAYING CARDS: A Pictorial History, Henry René D'Allemagne. Over 900 elaborate, decorative images from rare playing cards (14th–20th centuries): Bacchus, death, dancing dogs, hunting scenes, royal coats of arms, players cheating, much more. 96pp. 9¼ x 12¼. 29265-7

MAKING FURNITURE MASTERPIECES: 30 Projects with Measured Drawings, Franklin H. Gottshall. Step-by-step instructions, illustrations for constructing hand-some, useful pieces, among them a Sheraton desk, Chippendale chair, Spanish desk, Queen Anne table and a William and Mary dressing mirror. 224pp. 8⅛ x 11¼.
29338-6

THE FOSSIL BOOK: A Record of Prehistoric Life, Patricia V. Rich et al. Profusely illustrated definitive guide covers everything from single-celled organisms and dinosaurs to birds and mammals and the interplay between climate and man. Over 1,500 illustrations. 760pp. 7½ x 10⅛. 29371-8

Paperbound unless otherwise indicated. Available at your book dealer, online at www.doverpublications.com, or by writing to Dept. GI, Dover Publications, Inc., 31 East 2nd Street, Mineola, NY 11501. For current price information or for free catalogues (please indicate field of interest), write to Dover Publications or log on to www.doverpublications.com and see every Dover book in print. Dover publishes more than 500 books each year on science, elementary and advanced mathematics, biology, music, art, literary history, social sciences, and other areas.